KESHAV BHIKAJI DHAWAE
SHREESAMARTHA-SADAN
GIRGAUM.BOMBAY

केशव भिकाजी ढवळे
श्रीसमर्थ - सदन
गिरगांव, मुंबई

केशव भिकाजी ढवळे जन्म शताब्दी
१८८२ - १९८२

भारत-गौरव ग्रंथमाला

श्रीसमर्थ सदन - प्रकाशन

— २४ —

The Karnatak Press Saga

BY THE SAME AUTHOR

The Future of the Indian Youth
Nirmal and Other Poems

The Karnatak Press Saga

Sadanand Bhatkal

Popular Prakashan
www.popularprakashan.com

Popular Prakashan Pvt. Ltd.
301, Mahalaxmi Chambers
22, Bhulabhai Desai Road
Mumbai 400 026

ISBN : 978-81-7991-554-7
(4302)

First Edition
July 2009

Illustrations and Cover Design by Bal Thakur

Printed by
Madhav D. Bhagwat
Mouj Printing Bureau
Khatauwadi, Girgaum
Mumbai 400 004

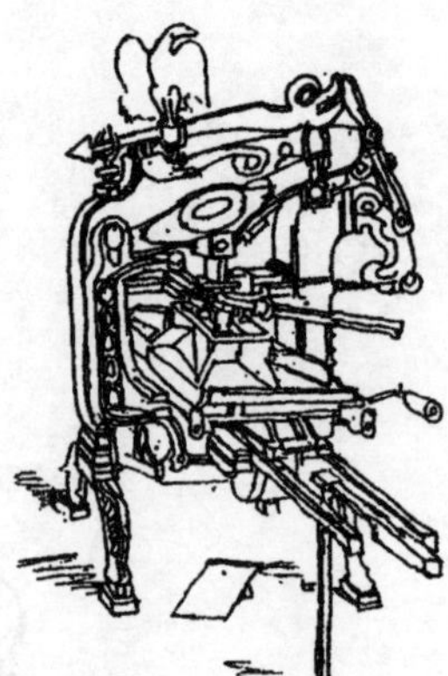

To
All the builders of
Karnatak Printing Press
Karnatak Type Foundry
and
Karnatak Publishing House

*

Contents

Preface

The centenary celebrations of 'Keshav Bhikaji Dhawale' was an event that did us – the bookmen of Maharashtra –proud. The firm, a family concern, was started in 1900 and the year 1999-2000 was celebrated by the present management of the firm by holding various functions during the year.

I have the habit of participating in such celebrations in more than a casual manner. Earlier too, a few such events were organized by me, some individually and others by taking a few friends along with me. While the official finalé was scheduled for July 2000, I suggested to a few of my friends that I as a booklover, should also felicitate the firm on this occasion. We decided to form a committee to chalk out the details.

Because of my emotional attachment to 'Karnatak' and because from 1945 'Karnatak' was a part of the Dhawale unit, I suggested that the Committee be called "Karnatak-Keshav Bhikaji Dhawale Centenary Celebrations Committee". I strongly believed and still feel that Karnatak did contribute to Dhawale's growth in a big way – a fact generally acknowledged by B. G. Dhawale (Sonyabapu), the Supremo of Dhawale-Karnatak in the issue of *Marathichiye Nagari* produced in 1949. Most of the members agreed to this suggestion and letterheads were printed accordingly. But some members of the Dhawale family took serious objection to thus name the Committee.

They asked me a question. "Can you tell us when

Karnatak was established?"

I had no reply to this question and even today it is difficult to authentically set any definite date of its establishment. The question was legitimate. We decided to drop the word Karnatak.

The history of the Dhawales and their work in the field of publishing, has been recorded in four publications published on different occasions. However, Karnatak, an important part of the Dhawale unit for decades, has not received due share of its achievements in the knowledge industry. It was necessary to do some research for getting data and record the history of nearly 125 years.

I decided to work on this project. However, I could not start work on this project till 2004, as till then I was fully occupied with the work on the three-volume *Sankshipta Marathi Wangmaya Kosh*, the last volume of which was released in mid-2003. While on that project I had the energy and enthusiasm to work on it and could carry it to a successful conclusion, I could not work on this quest with the same physical strength because of my ill-health. Though I had one or two projects in my mind, the quest for Karnatak took precedence.

I remembered vaguely a reference to *Kannada Suvarte* in P.B.Kulkarni's book *Nirnay Sagarchi Akshar Sadhana* and also some information about this journal in *Chitrapur Saraswat Directory*. This became the starting point. As the Kannada journal had ceased publication over a century ago, I sought the help of my friend Dr. Sreenivas Havnur, former Librarian of Tata Institute of Fundamental Research, Mumbai, and later Head of Kannada Department of University of Bombay. He had given a lot of data in his book which was extremely helpful and I have taken the liberty of extensively quoting from that exceedingly useful tome.

Let me state at the outset that it was a more arduous task

than what I had bargained for. It took me two years to collect some of the material for this tiny book. Going back to the events of the nineteenth century was not an easy task. The breakthrough came from Dr. Sreenivas Havnur, as stated above, who provided me with valuable data.

In the first place, my health did not keep in tune with my mental ruminations. Age had caught up and sapped my strength considerably. Ataxia, with which I have been affected, further slowed down my progress. But the most disturbing feature was the absence of data which could give an authentic picture of the last 125 years of this Institution's history. I had thought that relatives and those associated with the families who managed Karnatak, would provide sufficient material which could be relied upon to write the history. As mentioned earlier, except for four 'commemoration' volumes published on special occasions by Keshav Bhikaji Dhawale, we drew a blank. I had personally seen a large number of documents at 'Karnatak House' during my frequent visits there. There was a record of every Karnatak/Dhawale manuscript. So also many agreements regarding properties etc. Unfortunately they were all disposed of by Sonyabapu Dhawale just a few months before he shifted from Marol to Pune. This was only a few months before his demise. Because of the physical ailments and mental agony that he was going through just a few months before his demise, he must have decided not to consult anyone at that time. The entire 'wealth' went to the store of a scrap dealer.

The loss to us can be noted by citing just two facts. With the lot, went two large-sized bust portraits of the Kulkarnis – Ganpat and Mangesh. More importantly, we lost file copies of all the publications which were carefully preserved by them. Among the publications, the two notable books, *New History of Marathas* by G.S. Sardesai and *Indian War of Independence* by Swantantryaveer V.D. Savarkar can be found (and that too, rarely) in some libraries. In some libraries, only reprints can be found. But to appreciate the brilliance of the first editions published by Karnatak, there can be no alternative but to view the file copies of these publications with the publishers. Normally, libraries remove the jackets and a much-handled library book cannot give you the feel of the publisher's imaginative production values.

Another factor which I wanted to bring into this study, was the management of such institutions by individual family businesses in contrast to corporate management. It would have really been an interesting study, as there are few such instances where they have such a long life as in the case of Karnatak – over 125 years.

Here is a case that presents to us representatives of a fourth generation carrying the flag aloft. My personal association with the Popular Group – again a family business – which at present is in the hands of representatives of a third generation of the family, prompted me to review the parallel cases. I do not feel that I was able to even touch the fringe of the issue in this small book. It is because I feel I was not equal to this daunting assignment. Still from the little analyses I have presented here, perhaps someone in the future will be able to make it a subject of his research and study.

I know I have not been able to do an in-depth study of the contribution this great Institution has made in our cultural life. I hope that I have been able to give a glimpse of the same.

*

Acknowledgements

Dr. S. Devadas Pillai, P.N. Kumtha, Sharad Gogate, Jaya Dadkar and Raghunath Gokarn have always supported me in all my endeavours. They have been extremely helpful this time also.

In a research-oriented undertaking like this, you need help from many persons. Some of those who provided me with useful information from time to time, were Sudhir Moodbidri, Gurunath Gokarn, Dr.Sunanda Karnad, Dinkar Nadkarni, Chitra Shirali, Ashok Dayanand Nadkarni, Sriniketan Sharad Gogate and Raghuvir Dhawale. Soniya Khare helped me to suitably copy-edit the manuscript.

Usha Takalkar willingly undertook to write the Marathi version of this story in her lucid style.

I am also grateful to Dr. Aroon Tikekar, Vasant Sarawate and P. G. Burde, who gave me valuable guidance whenever I had difficulty.

I thank Vaishali Katale and Atul Joshi who helped me initially to prepare the manuscript. Thanks are also due to Madhav Bhagwat of Mouj who has been of much help at all stages of production of the book and Bal Thakur who has provided the sketches.

I am extremely grateful to all the above-mentioned friends, who made it possible for me to write this 'Saga'.

–Sadanand Bhatkal

Histories make men wise; poets, witty; the mathematics, subtle; natural philosophy, deep; moral, grave; logic and rhetoric, able to contend.

–Francis Bacon

1

Prologue

This is the story of Karnatak Press, which was founded sometime in the latter half of the nineteenth century and through its many avatars has served the literary needs of the people of the country for nearly a century and a quarter.

We have described it as a 'saga'. The Oxford Dictionary describes 'saga' as a long traditional story of heroic adventures, chronicling the account of members of a family or "social group". Our story spans three generations, but of three different families, who made noteworthy contributions in the field of knowledge. The story will begin with the pioneers, the Nadkarnis, bringing it up to 1896; moving on to the second family, the Kulkarnis, who nurtured the institution and took it to its pinnacle up to 1945, and thereafter, finally to the Dhawales.

It is not just the history of an institution but also a record of some facts of economic life in the western part of India over the last century and a half.

Notionally, the period of our story may be divided into almost equal time-frames – the earlier one, of a little less than 60 years up to 1945, when the unit was under the control or management of Nadkarnis and Kulkarnis and the latter, of a little over 60 years, when the Dhawales monitored it. The first can be described as the pragmatic group while the second as more impetuous, a little moody or temperamental. It can also be divided into more or less the pre- and post-independence eras of Indian history. Of course, the situations do not change dramatically but there certainly are perceptual influences in these two different time-frames. Speaking about the basic character of the managerial team we should remember that there are no rigid and watertight attitudes or approaches because one does get influenced by people, circumstances and situations that surround them.

It is true that today few people will remember Karnatak in its original avatar and very few know that its career started as printers and publishers of a nationalistic paper and later developed into a full-fledged "Book Unit" where work was undertaken almost on a turnkey basis – from editing to the finished product. Today the Karnatak banner has a token presence in the form of occasional publishing.

It was felt that the achievements of Karnatak should be documented not just because of the many commendable services that it rendered but also because a study of those diverse personalities who were at the helm of Karnatak, their approaches and all the actions and results that accompanied them, present an interesting set of events and a thrust that can help students of management studies in many ways. In a sense this is a case study by itself.

Originally, Karnatak started as Karnatak Press; later it had at least three distinct units under it – Karnatak Printing Press, Karnatak Publishing House and Karnatak Type Foundry. These units served another publisher of equal repute, Keshav Bhikaji Dhawale who took over

Karnatak in 1945. In pre-independent India such "mergers" or "collaborations" were unthinkable. But incidentally (one may call it providentially) these did come about and we shall try to note their implications to the extent possible. One of the advantages we have in such an attempt is that a few studies are available in regional languages (in Marathi and Kannada) which provide some data. We can find some references in official and private sources which are available for making this study possible. But the unit Karnatak has such a turbulent history that it becomes difficult to narrate its progress or regress from time to time, as succinctly as we would like to do. The managers had such different motives, varied ambitions and diverse styles of functioning that it is impossible to look at Karnatak as one solid monolithic institution.

This is a story of a 125 year old institution and it becomes difficult on occasions to ascertain the accuracy of details, especially about the dates of events and happenings.Written material available about some of the events that we are dealing with raises many doubts. Many times these writers who certainly are scholars of repute, give information which when considered with other evidence is confusing, often making you doubt the credibility of their findings. They must have made efforts to collect data as accurately as possible just as we have attempted to do. Some of the confusing evidence will be clear to our readers as we have indicated the variants at the relevant places in the narrative.

There are reasons for undertaking the writing of this book. The first one is to acknowledge the work of the pioneers in this profession as well as their contributions to the development of a facet of our national life which has been described by reputed scholars as an 'era' in itself.

The second reason is to inform the readers about the work and achievements of these pioneers. It was felt that very few of the present generation have knowledge of this eventful period and though there is a dramatic change in technology and approach in the three fields of knowledge in which the subjects of our book worked, namely, journalism, printing and publishing, there is a lot to learn from their working methods, their idealism, their endeavours, achievements and also from their misadventures.

Karnatak and Bhatkals have a close relationship of over nine decades. It began when the founder of Popular Book Depot, Ganapatrao Bhatkal served Karnatak Press for a short period, a little after he passed his school final, the Matriculation, in 1914. However, the relationship has, over the decades, been cemented in more than one form; as booksellers, customers, clients and publishers, as a friend in need and above all as well-wishers, who have collaborated with them in many ways. All these roles will feature in our story. So, let us proceed with our narrative.

We now 'switch on' the time machine and put it in reverse gear to the nineteenth century.

2

Bankikodla and...

We go back in time by 150 years. The locale is the west coast of India. Coasts and coastal towns anywhere in the world present a delightful environment. That is why those who live away from such an environment think of a trip to these places, at least occasionally, to enjoy nature's bounty present there. The beaches are expansive. Whether you are sitting on the golden sands or slumbering there, you can hear the sound of the little ripples when the sea is calm or the roar of the mighty waves when the sea is turbulent. Both the sounds are enthralling. In the hamlets and tiny towns around, one observes scenes which would be a delight to painters, photographers, poets and all creative artists. Little cottages with thatched roofs and some with tiled roofs of the more affluent amidst splendid colourful flora is a picturesque scene of the dwellings. Greenery of all shades; bushes, thickets, tall palms soaring high to converse with the clouds or huge rain trees or corn trees sheltering swallows, kites, parrots and all kinds of birds. On the ground, insects would be an entomologist's delight for research. The brownish red or blackish brown roads add to the colour to the scenario.

We have earlier referred to the Chitrapur Saraswat community. It is a community that is comparatively small

Part of Bankikodla - a quiet, fairly prosperous town in Uttar Kannada

in number, estimated to have not more than 30,000 individuals at present, which sought to have its own identity in the early eighteenth century, 300 hundred years ago, in 1708 to be precise. It makes an interesting story to record; but before we come to that we may look at an aspect of the Hindu society that presents a dilemma of a sort, at least to the present writer. This society has over the millennia split into *varnas, jatis,* castes and numerous sub-castes. One explanation that is offered for such a phenomenon is that Hindus are accommodative, tolerant and therefore there is full liberty to individual groups to define their own identity. As a matter of fact, the large Hindu pantheon is also of a similar nature. How and why so many *devas* and their consorts, or even their charioteers were necessary when the religion itself seeks to stress the oneness of the Universe (Advait) is not very easy to comprehend. Even assuming the reasons described by Sir James George Fraser in his *The Golden Bough* as valid, they are not enough to explain the variety in the Hindu pantheon. One can only surmise that the early Hindu society had poets of immense imagination and creativity. Even after their splendid description in detail about the five elements, they retained enough imagination to create *devatas* – perhaps as symbols of different aspects of human nature and their aspirations – and to make them so acceptable in form and attributes that their creations have fascinated all and sundry, not excluding the non-believers. To take just one or two examples we can speak of :

Ganesha :

The Lord of Wisdom : While Shiva and Parvati assumed the form of monkeys and enjoyed themselves in the forest, Parvati got pregnant and Shiva took the semen from the womb and gave it to Vayu (wind God). Vayu deposited it in the womb of Anjana, who delivered a son named Hanuman. Shiva assumed the form of an elephant (tusker) and Parvati that of a she-elephant. Parvati delivered a son in the form of an elephant. That son was named Ganesha or Ganapati.

Saraswati :

"By this single song, may they be strung together
All, small and big. In this tiny world.
May happiness lie forever at thy tender feet,
Like a garland, singularly unique!

May thou be the inmost inmate of my mind:
With graceful poise; charming figure;

Fair complexion; beautiful smile;
Veena in hand – thou, holder of *Veena* !

Continuously revolving are the sun, moon and stars;
Aeon after aeon, like the whirl of human souls.
Beginning-less and primeval are these who voyage on
the ocean of thy music divine!
Then will I see, in Space, the Timeless One;
Hymning rhythmically to keep the time!
Also the Ten Damsels, with unbraided hair,
Dancing merrily in vast expanse!

Among the many laudable principles in Indian philosophy, the one that impresses us most is that which advises to shun ego and to be free from hatred and enmity etc.

The Bhagwad Gita says : "To action alone hast thou a right and never at all to its fruits; let not the fruits of action be thy motive; neither let there be in thee any attachment to inaction."

This famous verse contains the essential principle of disinterestedness. When we do our work, plough or paint, sing or think, we will be deflected from disinterestedness, if we think of fame or income or any such motive, except the goodwill, the willing fulfilment of the purpose of God. Success or failure does not depend on the individual but on other factors as well. Giordano Bruno says: "I have fought that is much, victory is in the hands of fate."

I feel that the splitting up of the society into numerous sub-castes is more due to personal factors and also because of the socio-economic realities that prompt one group of persons to dominate over the other or because of avaricious intentions of securing economic benefits or just greed for power. The present plethora of political parties is also the result of such psyche among the leaders (?) of such parties – splitting further all the time on the slightest pretext, but mostly based on personal ego or for economic gains.

Saraswat Brahmans are part of Brahmans who were originally descendants of the Aryan invaders who came to Kashmir. Later they migrated to almost all parts of India.

Some of them established temples and settled down, serving in the Government administration or as small chieftains of the area, or as small land owners. One section of these, namely, Goud Saraswat Brahmans came over to Goa and built a few temples at Kushastali and Kelushi. Even today the Saraswat Brahmans, wherever they may be, do visit these temples as often as they can. Surprisingly, however modern or liberal the members of these families, they will have a photograph of their *kuldaivata,* the family deity – Mangesh or Shantadurga– in their homes.

In 1708 or thereabout a dispute arose in the Nagar kingdom, about 75 miles from Goa, over the incumbent as Chief Advisor to the Raja. Already the Saraswat Brahmans were split into two groups – Shaivaites* and Vaishnavaites*. The Shankaracharya of Shringeri Math (monastery) happened to be the overall pontiff among these Saraswat Brahmans. Besides the Shringeri Math Saraswat Brahmans had Maths (monasteries) at Kavale, Kashi, Udipi, not to speak of several other smaller Maths scattered all over the Konkan region where Saraswat Brahmans had settled right up to South Malabar, presently part of Kerala.

---

* Shaivaites - followers of Shiva. Vaishnavaites - followers of Vishnu. Vaishnavaite Saraswats' *math* is at Udipi.

The dispute referred to above took a serious turn when one group amongst the Saraswat Brahmans accused the other when one from the group was selected to the post of Chief Advisor of the Raja. They contended that they had no status in the society as they had no guru of their own. We are told the leaders of this group who were thus challenged prayed insistently for eight days and implored the deity at the small temple at Koteshwar in Gokarn. Their prayers were answered by *akashwani* (Divine pronouncement) and they did find one guru. Thus a new Jati came into existence. When this happened the members of the group had actually settled in the northern part of Kanara and the Math was established in Gokarn. It was only later that they got the land and premises at Chitrapur, a village near the Venkatapur river; midway between the two important towns of Kanara, namely, Mangalore and Karwar.

Dr. Frank Conlon, Professor of History at the University of Washington, has made an in-depth study of this community in his book *A Caste in a Changing World : The Chitrapur Saraswat Brahmans, 1700-1935*. It is a well-documented thesis on the birth, the growth and the progress of this community. However, this research work does not answer many questions we face. What exactly was the need for a separate identity for this group? In fact, what do we mean by "the group"? Till the split occurred in 1708 the two were one. Yet how did they claim a separate 'culture' as their own? The Chitrapur Saraswat Brahmans have somehow got a distinctive epithet 'Bhanap'. Various explanations have now been offered, but none of them is convincing enough to explain this epithet. But this need not worry us. They call themselves more plausibly, 'amchis' which means 'our brotherhood'. And thus there is talk of a separate 'bhanap culture,' whatever that means.

These 'amchis' did not come together at one stroke. For example, the first heroes of our story the Nadkarnis were supposed to have joined this group much later. Rao Bahadur S.S. Talmaki in his painstaking book *Saraswat Families* (1935) writes:

"The Saraswats who left Goa for good, whether during the period of the Inquisition or before or after, have carried certain links to bind them to their old homes in Goa. These will be detailed hereafter, but two of them which relate to the history of the community deserve a place here. These are the two surnames Kulkarni and Nadkarni. They require some notice as they are closely connected with Goa Saraswats. The affix 'karani' in the case of both these words is an abbreviated form of the Kanarese word 'Karanika' which means a writer. The word 'Kulkarani' now pronounced as Kulkarni, is the older of the two. 'Kula' means a community or a communal stock as in the case of the word 'Kula-deva'. The word Kulkarni was first applied to the writer or accountant of the village community which was a very old institution in Goa, being at one time found in every village of standing. Many of these institutions are still allowed to continue by the Portuguese Government under the name of 'communidades'. One interesting point to be noted in connection with these Kulkarnis, while working under the village communities, is that they maintained their records in Kannada script but in the local Marathi or Konkani language. Only a few such specimens are now available and some of these can be seen in the old records of the Mangeshi temple. The system of writing Marathi and Modi characters came into

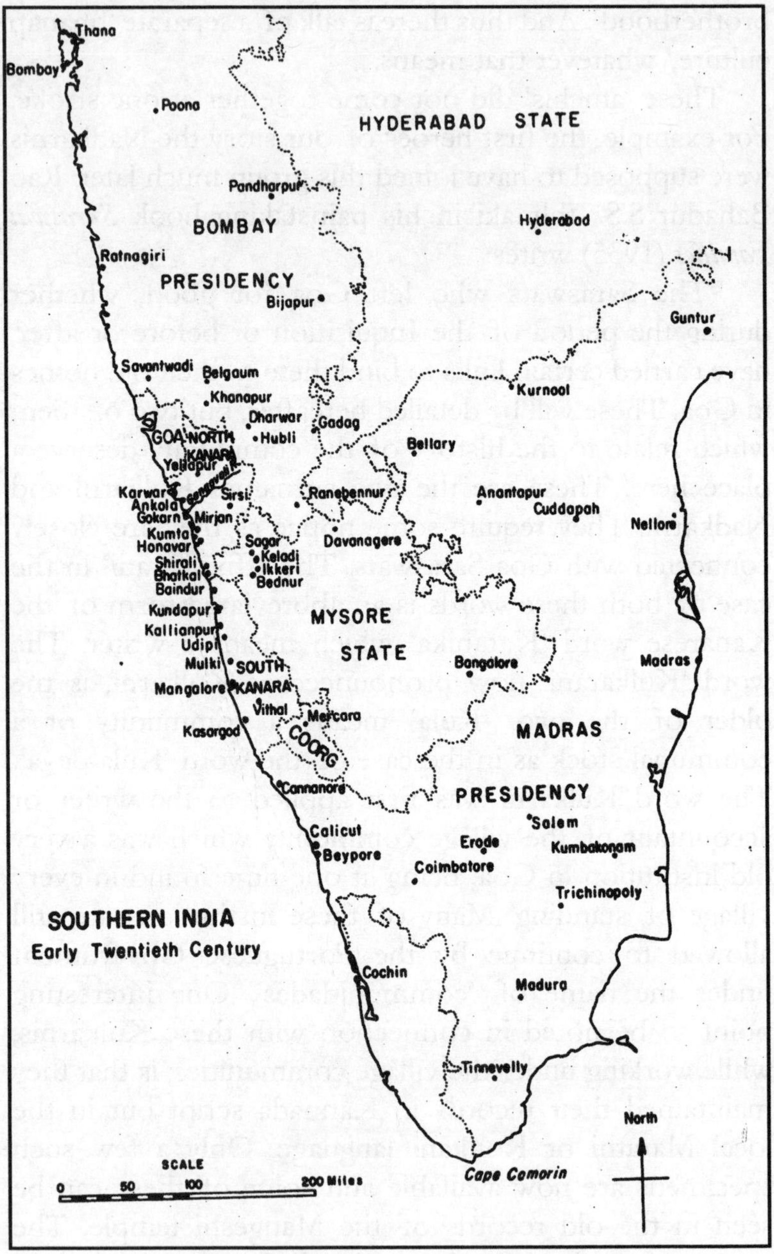

Southern India in the early twentith century

vogue in Goa after the province had come under the influence of the Marathas. When the Chalukyas began to rule in Goa, the village accountant appointed by Government was called Kulkarni and the word came into use with that significance in Maharashtra also which too was then ruled by the Chalukyas. The village accountant continued to be called by the same name under later kings, as also under British rule. In the Kanarese country including Kanara* and Mysore the term for village accountant is Shanabhoge or Shanbhaga, except in that part of Karnatak which is close to Maharashtra. In the Ghat districts adjoining Kanara the term Shanabhoge is used for a village accountant. Nadkarni is an officer appointed to keep accounts of the whole district and the name is derived from 'Nad' meaning a district. The word was in use only in Goa and that too during the time of the Chalukyas and did not travel beyond that province. In the Kanarese districts the corresponding word used is Nadguda and Nadiga. In any case the office has ceased to exist under the British rule. It may be noted that Kulkarni as a surname is in use, so far as Brahmans are concerned, among the Saraswats including those in Kanara and among the Deshasthas of Kolhapur. As for Nadkarni, it is used as a surname only by the Saraswats of Goa including those who have settled in Kanara, and its source can only be traced to Goa."

Most of these families were land owners and some took up service with the government. Talmaki has

* Bhanaps came to Goa from the north first and later migrated to the south of the region. They were mostly in Karwar (now in Uttar Kannada District), which was administered from Bombay (now Mumbai) then headquarters of the Bombay Presidency and in Mangalore (now in Dakshin Kannada District), which was administered from Madras (now Chennai), the headquarters of the Madras Presidency.

reported that at the time of the compilation of *Saraswat Families* he could trace 504 families.This work is being updated. But yet no study of the family names has been made so far. If and when this is undertaken it may throw some light on various socio-cultural (perhaps even economic) reasons for the emergence of such an exclusive community. It certainly will be an interesting story and perhaps instructive too, from a sociological point of view.

Most of the Chitrapur Saraswat Brahmans were scattered along the coast of what is known as the Kanaras. Under the British regime, administratively the region underwent a lot of re-adjustments of territory. But basically the Chitrapur Sasraswat Brahmans stayed in towns of North and South Kanaras. In the North, Kumta and Honaver were the main places around which a number of them congregated. These two towns were very important ports and a lot of export and import trade was done through these ports. Obviously some families must have also worked with the trading community; one such, N.A. Sirur and Co. was in cotton trading and textiles, and later expanded their business in far-off places like Bangalore and Bombay. Others took to some professions and a few others owned land and as we have already noted the rest went into government service.

Nadkarni denotes a position of a revenue officer, just as Kulkarni too denotes another position in the revenue department. It is said that Kulkarnis were also perhaps entrusted with the records of births and deaths. However, they were working in a smaller area while Nadkarnis were responsible for the entire *prant*. Incidentally Nadkarnis form the bulk of the Chitrapur Saraswat Brahamans, largely settled around a convenient place called

Bankikodla, just about 14 kilometres away from Kumta. This place was popularly called Vilayat (meaning England) of Bhanaps, suggesting that it was the place for the elite having numerous advantages. It was proximate to places famous for pilgrim centres like Gokarn, Kotiteerth and not far from the district town of Karwar. Bhanaps staying in Bankikodla and Gokarn had the vision to see that the area at Sanikatta could be developed into salt pans and any investment in the area will bring lucrative dividends for years to come. The Sanikatta Salt Co-operative Society Ltd. was founded by some of them. Subsequently it was also nursed and developed by Bhanaps.

It is necessary to note that the career they followed allowed them sufficient income, though not to amass a fortune, but certainly to invest in plots of land. Enterprising as they were they thought of projects like harvesting the salt pans, cotton trade etc. The cotton trade as we have noted earlier took some of them later further east to Hubli, Davangere, Chitradurg and other towns.

Another point that needs to be noted is the fact that Chitrapur Saraswat Brahmans were practical and pragmatic. This becomes relevant in the context of the 'bhanap culture' that is being talked about. Those who were in government service succumbed to temptations (like bribery, corruption) that are usual for persons in position of authority and power. Persons in trade were cunning as necessitated by circumstances. There is a report about the Sanikatta Salt Co-operative Society Ltd. founded in 1923. An independent report on the cooperative structure of this Society during that time, found out that it was an association or a society not in any way based on the principle of cooperative producers or

Shamrao Vithal Kaikini
(1841 - 1905)

consumers and it could not be called a genuine cooperative society but a syndicate of owners. Obviously the promoters of this Society were keen to receive all the benefits that were being given to the cooperative sector. (Even today, many such examples can be cited).

This discussion leads us to the family of Nadkarnis, the bulk of whom were residing in Bankikodla, not far away from Sanikatta. Even a casual study of the family data as compiled by Shripadrao Talmaki in his book, *Saraswat Families,* shows that in the eighteenth and early nineteenth centuries, Chitrapur Saraswat Brahmans had large families, each of them having on an average 6 or 7 children, some even a dozen or more. Apparently it was found necessary for members of such families to seek other opportunities for their very sustenance. They could not support themselves on their farms or other income. Nor were there enough jobs in the government or private enterprises. Many in that regional area had to migrate from their native towns and villages for livelihood and education too.

One such enterprising person was Shamrao Vithal Kaikini. He was the pioneer of the Saraswat community in Bombay and by sheer industry and application attained a position of considerable prominence. He was born in 1841 at Murdeshwar, a small village in the North Kanara district, pretty well-known for its salubrious climate. His father Vithalrao Manjunathayya was a landlord and a government servant. Shamrao received his early school education in Murdeshwar and Honavar, but the facilities for the study of English being then very few, he was apprenticed to gentlemen who were known to possess some knowledge of it. He passed the English (Grade I) Public Service Examination and then entered the Revenue Department as a clerk in 1859 under Mr. (later Sir) William Wedderburn, Assistant Collector of the district. In 1864 he paid his first visit to Bombay, and after serving for some months as a clerk to Shantaram Narayan Patkar, a very prominent pleader of the High Court, returned to his post in the Revenue Department. In 1866 Mr. (later Sir) Raymond West, the District Judge of Kanara, took him over as a clerk in his office. Soon after, he was specially entrusted with the work of translating documents and papers in connection with cases which were pending in appeal before the Privy Council. This work brought him again to Bombay in 1867, and he did it so satisfactorily that he was appointed the second Kanarese Translator and Interpreter in the High Court.

He remained at this post till 1871, when he appeared for and passed with credit the High Court Pleaders' examination. Soon after, he began practice on the Appellate side of the High Court and rose to prominence. Being for many years the only Kanarese-knowing pleader at the High Court, he was much in demand in the Appellate Courts of the Kanarese districts of Dharwar, Belgaum, Bijapur and Karwar. He died of plague at his residence at Santa Cruz in Bombay on 15 June 1905 at the age of 64. Shamrao became a legend in his own time, so much so that when Talmaki proposed to form a Cooperative Credit Society in 1906 he named the institution as Shamrao Vithal Cooperative Credit Society, now the Shamrao Vithal Cooperative Bank Ltd. People erroneously consider Shamrao Vithal as the founder of the Bank. Shamrao Vithal's contribution to the progress of those who accompanied him to Bombay or those who followed him later can be gauged from an interesting article titled "The Kanara Club, Bombay" written by V.V. Kalyanpurkar and S.N. Koppikar. It is worth reproducing the article *in toto* as it gives an account of the story of the three decades of life in Bombay of struggling young persons working in the growing city at that time.

> "In the early seventies of the last century, the absence of a High School in Kanara compelled a small band of enterprising and ambitious youths of the Saraswat community of North Kanara to leave their homes in pursuit of higher education. The first batch consisted of Messrs Anant Subrao Nadkarni (Haigund), Anant Venkatesh Samsi, Shantappa Manjunath Murdeshwar, Anant Shantappa Nadkarni (Budwantu), Narayan Shamrao Murdeshwar and Sheshgiri Subrao Murdeshwar.

Lokamanya Tilak at Shantaram's Chawl in Mugbhat, Girgaum

Their first destination was Ratnagiri where they underwent a High School course. By the time they finished their education at Ratnagiri, Bombay was gradually becoming more and more familiar to the students of the community owing to the generosity of Mr. Shamrao Vithal Kaikini which had already drawn to Bombay a few young men, the first and foremost among whom was the late Dr Sir Narayan Chandavarkar. The others were Messrs Durgappa Krishnayya Kaikini, Anandrao Timmappayya Gundil and Mangesh Devrao Nadkarni. The next step, therefore, of the Ratnagiri batch was to move northward to Bombay for further studies. On their arrival in Bombay they started a club for boarding and lodging, and named it 'The Kanara Club'. As these young men were strangers to Bombay, they located the club in the immediate neighbourhood of Mr. Shamrao Vithal's residence in Kandewadi and pursued their studies under the fostering care and kindness of that gentleman and his worthy wife Mrs Subhadrabai. The young students had to depend for their food upon local cooks whose way of cooking was quite different from

* *Keshav Bhikaji Dhawle's residence at Akshi*

their own and found the food prepared by them somewhat unpalatable. Mrs Shamrao Vithal quickly perceived their plight and relieved their discomfort by frequently inviting them to dinner on holidays and sometimes by arranging for oil-baths for those who wished to have them. That kind and philanthropic lady thus made them feel that they were not quite away from their own homes. The number of members of the club at this time was about ten, though there used to be temporary additions in the examination season. In 1877 the club suffered a severe loss in the death of Mrs Shamrao Vithal whose maternal solicitude for the welfare of its members is still remembered by the old members.

"Shortly after that unfortunate event, the club was

* Bankikodla and Akshi both are small towns very near to the west coast of India. Both these towns have an environment that promotes similar economic, cultural and social situations. The owners of Karnatak Press, the Nadkarnis and the Kulkarnis coming from Bankikodla and the Dhawales from Akshi is however, a mere coincidence.

A typical small town-well with 'Rahats', devices for drawing water

removed to Shantaram's Chawl in Mugbhat, when the infant club might be said to have reached the age of adolescence and became more widely known throughout Kanara. The membership also began to rise as, term after term, more boys – especially younger boys – began to flock in from their homes. Though Karwar had been blessed with a High School by this time, glowing accounts of the superior education imparted in the Bombay High Schools were reaching the ears of ambitious youths. And not all the persuasions of the Karwar Headmaster could prevent them from leaving his school – much to his chagrin – and running up to Bombay often in anticipation of their parents' sanction. One peculiar characteristic of the club at this time was that a good many members, senior in age and advancement, had juniors with them to take care of in the person of a younger brother or a nephew or a brother-in-law. The Koppikars, the Kalyanpurkars, the Kulkarnis, the Chickarmanes, the Balvallis and the Gangollis – each contributed a senior member and also one or two junior members of the family to the membership of the club. In some cases, the circumstance that the senior member was already in Bombay led his younger relation in Karwar to turn his eyes towards Bombay, while, in others both the seniors and the juniors were packed off together to Bombay by the parents in the often well-founded hope that the senior would make up for the previous neglect of his studies, and the junior would be safe under the tutelage and the restraining influence of his elder relation. There were also some elderly gentlemen as members of the club, who were employed in the government and mercantile offices and who also exercised a wholesome influence, even over the elder members of these groups, by their presence and advice. One of these gentlemen was Mr (now Dewan Bahadur) Venkatrao Yennemadi who, after a short stay in the club, set up an independent lodging close to the club rooms and continued to exercise the same influence on all the students of the club until he left Bombay to fill higher posts in the mofussil. A large number of members consisted of young lads fresh from their homes and were unaccustomed to the food prepared by the local cooks. But they soon found another kind lady in Mrs. Bijur Narayanrao whose husband too, after living in the club for some time when he used to entertain the students during dull hours with his sallies of wit and humour, took up, on her joining him, an independent lodging in the close neighbourhood of the club. Twice a week the kind lady permitted the club cook to take instructions from her in preparing those condiments (*tamblies* and *kadies*) which still remain the more popular and characteristically communal condiments of the Saraswats of Kanara. These condiments, dinners and oil-baths may perhaps appear to the present day reader as too small to be noticed in a writing of this kind. But, in the eyes of those that actually derived benefit from them, they still remain a vivid example of a generous and sympathetic effort to lessen the discomfort of new arrivals, to popularize the club and to attract to Bombay more young boys from Kanara who might otherwise lag behind.

"In short, the club at Shantaram's Chawl appeared more like a joint family concern where the elder members both by example and precept, showed the way, and the younger ones respectfully followed it. The members used to feel such a fond attachment to the club that even those that later on joined the college and resided in the college hostel, used to get their homesickness considerably relieved by spending a day or two weekly or fortnightly in the club without having had to pay for it. And, finally, the outstanding feature of the whole institution was the growth of a spirit of self-sacrifice and mutual sympathy and goodwill towards one another which was particularly noticeable in times of illness etc. of any member. A few well-to-do students joined the Elphinstone College which had a hostel, but the majority of the members attended the Wilson High School or the Wilson College (then known as the Free General Assembly's Institution) which had become a favourite with the Kanarites owing to the generous and sympathetic treatment meted out to them by the Revd. Doctor Mackichan and his colleagues. The Kanara Saraswat students owe a deep debt of gratitude to that reverend gentleman for his help in securing for some of them suitable employment after leaving his college.

"Life in the club at Shantaram's Chawl was on the whole simple and agreeable. While the monotony of the local food was relieved twice a week by *tamblies* and *kadies* and by the kind attentions of Mrs Bijur, there was nothing of extravagance or luxury. Most of the members, especially the juniors, had no separate rooms for study. There was only one small common hall where they sat and read during day and slept by night. The lights used were of pure cocoanut oil, the lamp being in the shape of a short glass tumbler with a wick floating in the middle of it on the surface of the oil. There were few chairs, and most of us sat on a mat to study. As for the dress – alas! Those days have gone, perhaps never to return – it was simple in quality and small in quantity. Two *dhotars* to be used on alternate days in the course of a whole year and two *pairans* with two coats to be washed alternately by the washerman, formed the whole wardrobe of a student. The coats were of kintan or of some black stuff of a kindred kind. They were long and without an open collar, and were modelled after the old Hindu fashion that prevailed then in Bombay. Collars and neckties were unknown. As regards the head-dress, the seniors wore a turban, while the juniors were content with a cap. In those days the turban had sometimes an advantage over the cap. A student wearing the former could easily get admission to a public lecture hall, while even his senior, if he happened to be in a cap, was often refused admission on the ground that the lecture was not meant for such young folk! The wearing of a turban was then regarded as a sign of gentlemanliness. But what a difference now! At present a booking clerk at a railway station or a steamer office is more courteous to a hatwalla asking for a third class ticket than to a gentleman in a turban asking for a first or second class ticket. Further, none of the members did his shaving himself. The barber was always requisitioned, and there was no shaving of the chin alone in the case of school or college students. The head too was shaved in the old Hindu fashion, and the domain of the tuft of hair was never permitted to be encroached upon by the 'crop'. The footwear bill rarely amounted to more than a rupee and a half a year. In fact, the average expenses, all told (excepting books and fees), of a student were below rupees fifteen a month. Taking tea at a public shop was rigidly disliked, and the only departure in that connection was an occasional purchase of a few *bajas* (bhajais), from the neighbouring shop of a Mangalorean to be used at the afternoon tea at the club. The justification for this departure probably lay in the circumstance that the Mangalorean had acquired a reputation for making excellently delicious *bajas*, so much so that even aristocratic gentlemen often asked to stop their coach and pair at this shop for a bundle of his *bajas*.

"An account of the Kanara club at Shantaram's Chawl will not be complete without a reference to the gadi or man-servant that was employed in its service. Rama gadi (for that was his name) was an elderly person, being older than the oldest member of the club. He was a faithful servant and regarded the club as his home. He was very affectionate and sympathetic in his own way, particularly to the junior members. As he was a well-meaning servant, the younger members often pocketed with much amusement his grandmotherly chat or card-play during vacations. He even claimed the privilege of chastising the cook for the latter's carelessness where the juniors were concerned. In a word, though himself a servant, he felt as if he was an elder member of the whole joint family. Indeed, he was not without his whims or defects. But they were of a trifling nature, and no one minded them in view of his good nature.

"During the year 1885, the club was removed to Krishnabai Buildings after a temporary occupation of a flat in Thakurdwar. From that date the club might be said to have reached the stage of full manhood. Facilities of steamer communication between Bombay and Kanara – both North and South Kanara – led to a rapid rise in the number of members which became so unwieldy as to necessitate a splitting up of the club into two parts for the sake of convenience and comfort. Both the clubs continued to pull on satisfactorily, and extended a warm welcome to all Saraswat members or visitors. There was at this time a slight change in the mode of life in the club. The distinction between a senior and a junior was no longer in evidence. The juniors as well as those of the seniors who still continued in the club, began to take an equal part in its administration. It may be mentioned that, for about ten years, the affairs of the club were managed mainly by Mr. Shankar Narayan Koppikar, and N. V. Kalyanpurkar, during his stay of many years in the club, laid the members under a debt of gratitude by his paternal care and sympathy. Sport now became more popular. A cricket club was formed under the guidance of Mr. Arur Mangeshrao who had already made his mark in the field of sport as one of the best wicket-keepers in the Hindu Gymkhana. Matches were played with other well-known teams. The club, however, had a short life of about five years (1885-1890). Food common to the Saraswat community became the order of the day owing to the employment of Saraswat cooks, though of a different sub-section. The dress also underwent a little change inasmuch as coats of superior quality and shirts with fixed collars instead of *pairans*, began to invade the student's wardrobe, though separate collars and neckties still remained outside his province. Taking tea or refreshments at a public shop slowly began to be regarded as permissible. The average expense of a student also increased. Better accommodation was provided for to ensure closer application to one's studies. But, while the majority of the members pursued their studies in right earnest, a few junior lads who had no elder relations in the club to guide or to restrain their tendency to idle away their time, were charged with paying less attention to their studies than what the sacrifices made by their parents in supporting them in Bombay desired. The lights used included a few kerosene oil lamps with globes.

"There was a further change in the conditions of Bombay in the beginning of the nineties. The number of Saraswat families that came to reside in Bombay multiplied rapidly. And many a student found it both economical and convenient to reside with such families instead of in the club. The old college hostels too expanded, and new ones were opened, which in the very nature of things, afforded greater facilities to the students to apply themselves more closely to their studies. The result was that the number of members of the club gradually decreased till it was broken up about the year 1892, being no longer necessary for the purpose for which it was originally started."

The epidemic of plague that rocked the city of Bombay during the last decades of the nineteenth century claimed thousands of lives. The Kanara Club was also one of the victims of this scourge.

As reported in the article reproduced above, Anant Nadkarni who was one of the beneficiaries of the munificence and patronage of the Kanara club, and his younger brother Mangesh, are the two persons connected with our story of the Karnatak Press.

3

The Beginning

It is not possible to give the exact date of the establishment of the Karnatak Press. A few scholars who have written about the printing and publishing history of Marathi books have given varying dates. Our search takes us to the eighth decade of the nineteenth century. In the archives of the Government of Maharashtra, we have gone through "Annual Reports on Native Papers" submitted by vigilant officers of the Government to their senior authorities who were in charge of watching, controlling or prohibiting seditious literature from the periodicals. These not only list the periodicals published at the time but also give the summaries of the major news and views by the journals. I have found a reference to *Kannada Suvarte* in the 1882 Annual Report. There is a reference to this journal in the *Chitrapur Saraswat Directory* (1933) as follows:

'*The Kannada Suvarte,* the *Mitrodaya* and the *Sudarshan* of the eighties of the last century and the *Suvasini* and *The West Coast Spectator* which flourished towards the end of it, are now but dim memories of a distant past. The only magazines owned and managed by Chitrapur Saraswats today are two namely *Kanara Saraswat* started in April 1919 as the organ of the Kanara Saraswat Association, Bombay and *Soma* a quarterly started by Mr.K.S.Bhat in London in 1931."

Both these references are with regard to *Kannada Suvarte.* Mangesh Santapa Nadkarni, who at one place is mentioned as an agent of *Kannada Suvarte*, is mentioned as an editor in another place. I reproduce the masthead of the issue of *Kannada Suvarte* of 1893 which clearly mentions that the journal was printed at the Karnatak Press.

Unfortunately I could not obtain more details about the address etc. However, it clearly indicates that the Karnatak Press was able to print at that time literature (material) in English, Kannada, Marathi and Gujarati. Thus the Press did exist in 1882. It is possible that perhaps it was set up sometime even before this date. We have the authentic records of publications issued in Marathi which list books and periodicals published up to 1950 in what is famously known as *Date Suchi.* It mentions at least 13 titles printed by Karnatak Press before 1900. In this compilation, the editors have stated that they have recorded only those books which they were able to lay their hands on. It is likely that the Press may have printed and released more literature apart from printing journals or publicity material in Marathi, besides whatever they printed in other languages. One interesting piece of information that we have obtained from this encyclopedia is a mention of Anant Nadkarni, the elder brother of Mangesh as publisher of a commentary on Bhagawat Gita released in 1887 by Jeevan Mukta Swami.

Biographical details of the two brothers, Anant and Mangesh, are almost unavailable. I had to piece together the scattered data available from other sources and make our own surmises to record the progress of the Karnatak

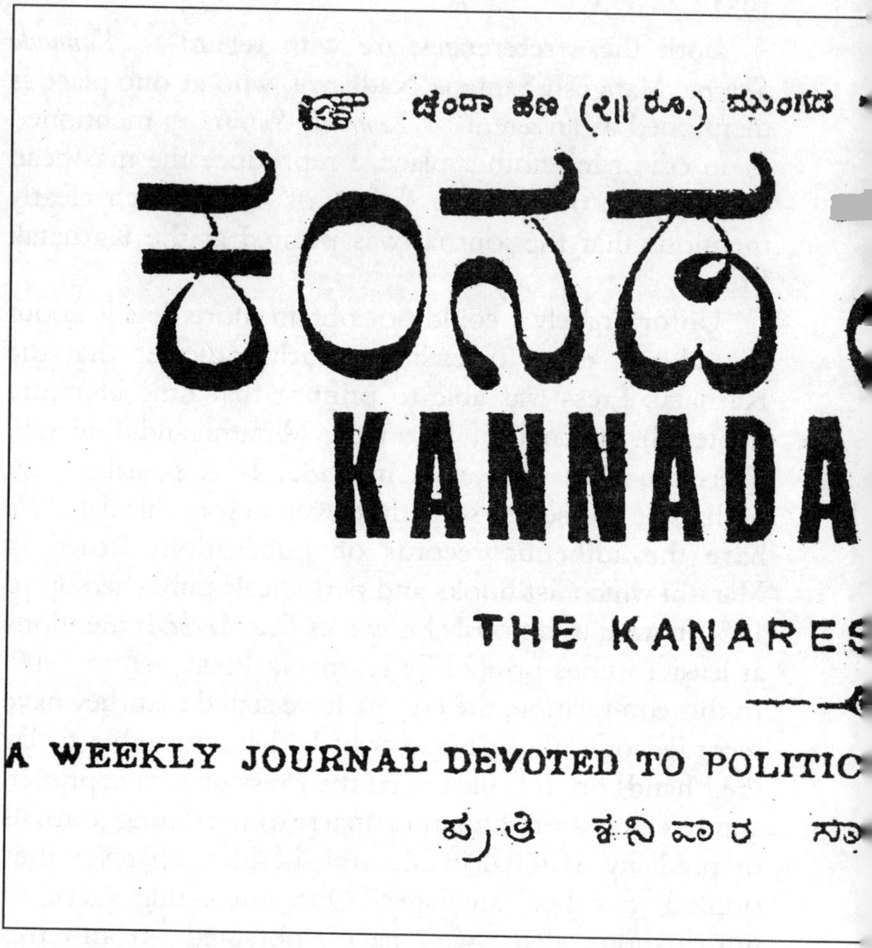

Masthead of Kannada Suvarte
A Weekly Journal devoted to Politics, Literature, Commerce, Science & Art

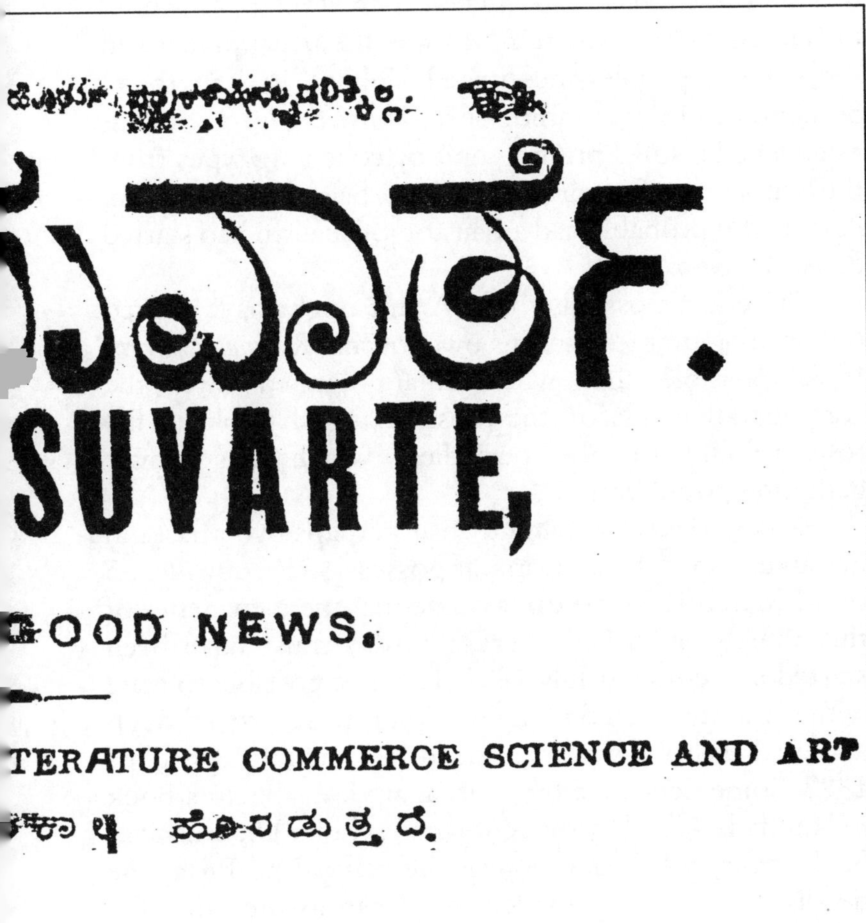
SUVARTE,

GOOD NEWS.

TERATURE COMMERCE SCIENCE AND ART

Press during this period. Apparently Anant the elder brother came to Bombay, spending a few years at a school in Ratnagiri, (as many did). As was the usual practice in those days, people encouraged siblings to join them. Sometime in 1880 or earlier, he may have come to Bombay, established a small printing unit by collecting types from the famous type foundries like Nirnay Sagar Press. By then, Anant who probably had a flair for journalism had started *Kannada Suvarte.*

There is a possibility that Anant might have started the printing unit to print his own journal *Kannada Suvarte.* It is possible that while Anant looked after the administrative side of the press, Mangesh took up the responsibility of the periodical which was slowly gathering popularity.

Kannada Suvarte apparently had perhaps two phases in its career. Since the issue in our possession is copy No. 35 of 11 March 1893, we can assume that the New Series of this weekly published every Saturday must have been started sometime in July 1892. It is not possible to state with certainty when the original Series was started though as stated earlier it was mentioned in "Annual Report" of 1882. Some details of the journal are available in a book in Kannada edited by the renowned scholar Dr. Sreenivas K. Havnur, titled *Hosa Kannadada Arunodaya.* From the details that he has provided me, I can assume that the strong editorials may have attracted the wrath of the Government and the journal might have ceased publishing temporarily and was restarted in June 1892. I am not sure whether it remained in circulation till the difficult period of the 1896 plague when the negotiations for the transfer of the Press to the new management started.

Before we come to the 1896 plague havoc it is

necessary to reproduce what Dr. Havnur has analyzed about the *Kannada Suvarte*. A free rendering of the matter follows:*

"From the year 1882 with the publication of *Hitabodhini* (Banglore), *Chandrodaya* (Dharwad) and *Kannada Suvarte* (Bombay), the profession of Kannada journalism took a new turn which is an awareness of thought process, independent expression of views along with national ethos.

Before these journals, *Karnatak Prakashika* and *Shodhak* also had followed the same path. However, it was more of individual contributions. Through the publication of the above three periodicals, journalism took roots as a tradition.

The editors of *Hitabodhini*, namely, M B Shreenivas Iyengar and M S Puttana, contributed to the prose of new Kannada language, which we have noted. This journal became a conduit for their work. Their aim in publishing it was research-oriented as explained below.

"Awareness makes people happy. Through *Hitabodhini* we have tried to bring out thought process among the public to the extent possible. Apart from explaining our Shastras, the useful new shastra of English language also has been included in the journal from time to time. We have also included stories containing humour as well as moral stories."

The editorial task of this periodical which commenced from October 1883 was taken up by M Venkata Krishnayya from its seventh issue. In the fourth year the *Hitabodhini* continued to have the same ideals, i.e. Western Science, Government Systems, News from Bharat as well

---

* Though we are primarily concerned about *Kannada Suvarte*, we have reproduced Dr. Havnur's analysis extensively to have a comparative study of its contemporary periodicals.

as foreign countries and family news. Thanks to the high level of morality and boldness of expression of the editors this periodical reached very high quality of contents during its life of 10-12 years. In 1883 *Chandrodaya* a Saturday weekly commenced. It made its own niche even among the Marathi weeklies and also reflected the critical analysis of the policies of the Government, while covering the news pertaining to the people's lives. It thrived for more than two decades and became a part and parcel of the lives of the people of the Karnataka part of the Bombay Presidency. Its stand on political issues received high acclaim.

As a torchbearer of patriotism we have to consider *Kannada Suvarte.* The atmosphere of Bombay was congenial for its publication. When the English forces captured Burma, *Kannada Suvarate*, in its issue of 8 January 1886 criticized them. The maintenance cost of Burma of more than Rs 30,000 would be an additional burden on the Indians, was the concern it expressed. *Kannada Suvarte* criticized even the British Prime Minister Mr. Gladstone (5 and 26 February 1886).

In the issue dated 2 November 1889, the editor makes a reference to Prince Albert's visit to the Mysore State and makes an oblique reference sarcastically that "Mysore State spent thousands of rupees on this visit but did not consider appropriate to felicitate Charles Bradlaugh working tirelessly for the Indian National Congress in London."

The analysis of the Indian economy appeared very often in this weekly. Whenever there was an increase in taxation, in gold and silver prices, and also when the annual budget was presented, the *Kannada Suvarate* commented with concern (5 October 1888 and 5 April

1889). It also highlighted the absence of a single Indian in the Finance Commission appointed by the British Government. The financial exploitation of the Indian economy became the subject of a long essay in it. It also heavily criticized the Public Service Commission, the condition of jails and the laws on Secrecy of Government activities from time to time (9 February 1888, 31 May 1889 and 4 November 1889). *Kannada Suvarte* supported the newly-born Indian National Congress (INC). It pointed out the separatist movement of Muslims in 1889, expressed its concern for unity in the Indian National Congress while advising that Parsis should not encourage the separatist movement (17 May1888). It also analysed at length the Bradlaugh Bill and the Indian National Congress's response in its issue of 3 March 1890.

The happenings in Bombay Presidency were obviously important events covered by this weekly. It pointed out on 11 May 1888 the reduction in the salary of Mr. Moose by setting up an Observatory at Colaba. It suggested in another issue that either Shamrao Vithal Kaikini or Tirumala Inamdar should represent Bombay Karnatak in the Legislative Council. *Kannada Suvarte* wrote about the criticism levelled against the Viceroy Dufferin and Lansdowne, the-then Governor of Bombay, and Lord Reay, who it described as a generous man. However, whenever he was wrong the journal did not spare him.

It said that his speech during the convocation ceremony of Bombay University was totally ineffective from an academic point of view (25 January 1889). It gave due attention to even small matters in educational field of Bombay. For example, it advocated that Venka Rango

Katti, who was doing commendable work should not be retired. If it is inevitable R. H. Deshpande should take his place (9 December 1889). Even though *Kannada Suvarte* was being published from Bombay it reported the events and activities, problems of farmers, misdeeds of Government officers, from distant Talukas of Kanara Districts particularly North Kanara. This way the weekly which struggled hard for the well-being of people from Burma to Bhatkal, maintained a high quality of journalism. It had mature thinking and impartial viewpoint. Though there were not many Kannada-speaking people in Bombay, it was published for more than 10 years and its journalists deserve kudos.

The other weekly, which rose to similar heights, was *Havyak Subodh* which lived from 1885 to 1889. It also had very good circulation like that of *Kannada Suvarte,* around 1000, quite high in those times. In both the journals the reporting was mild. But both upheld patriotism. Their aim was the well-being of the people. In them we also find extensive news coverage and mature analysis. The pen of the editor of *Havyak Subodh*, Karla Venkatraman Shastri appears to be sharper. He had offered a suggestion even for the improvement of Forex Reserve ! He pointed out that there was a drain on the economy due to the large pay packets of British officials and suggested that henceforth Indian officials should be appointed.

It is recorded that the plague had taken a toll of nearly a crore of lives in India from 1896 to 1917. Among the few workers at the Karnatak Press there was an enterprising person named Ganpat Narayan Kulkarni. When the Nadkarnis thought of closing down the Press after most of the workers left Bombay during the epidemic, Ganpat was bold enough to suggest to the Nadkarnis that he would take it over from them. From the information that I have gathered, the Nadkarnis left Bombay and went back to their native place, Bankikodla. In the family tree Anant Nadkarni is also mentioned as "master". He started coaching students. He also ran a modest general provisions store in Bankikodla for some time.

4

1896-1916

Ganpat Narayan Kulkarni was a typesetter earning Rs. 6 per month when he ventured to suggest to his masters that instead of closing the Karnatak Press altogether it may be handed over to him. It was certainly a daring suggestion *per se*. It was decided that he would have to pay Rs. 4000 for the takeover. Though it was a difficult proposition he did not shirk and started on a mission to collect funds. It is obvious that though the deal was struck in 1896, some time must have lapsed for collecting the required amount. The successful quest for gathering funds would make an interesting study but unfortunately the sources of information are unavailable to us. We only know that amongst the few who helped this young man was Pannalal Jain, a wealthy person who owned several estates in the city. Many Saraswat Brahmans (Bhanaps) lived in the Pannalal Terrace building at Grant Road, Mumbai, at that time. They must have put in their word of recommendation to Pannalal. The reputation of the Press with its 'nationalist' leaning must also have played some part. Besides, Pannalal Jain must have had faith in the experience of this young man who had dared to enter this business. Though his own contribution is reported to be only Rs. 500, he would have helped Ganpat to collect the balance from other sources.

In any case it is possible that the actual ownership of the Press may have been passed on to him only in 1902 as in the intervening years Bombay faced the consequences of the plague epidemic. Also the question of making the full payment of the sum agreed upon was perhaps a factor in transferring the ownership. Again, as per the usual routine practice amongst Bhanaps, Ganpat asked his younger brother Mangesh to join him in Bombay. However, even before this happened Ganpat must have earned for himself a status and place in the civic society, especially among the Bhanap community not only as an industrious and enterprising person but also as one who deserved to be in the small group that met often to consider the problems of social and economic nature faced by the members of the community. We have already referred to the Kanara Club. It is possible that Ganpat may have actively participated in the compilation of *Chitrapur Panchang*, a directory of Bhanaps – a sort of census of those living in Bombay, published in 1896. The group that was involved in the community activities included businessmen like Kundapur Anandrao and his son, and respected leaders like Shamrao Vithal Kaikini and Shripad Talmaki who deservedly earned the sobriquet as the pioneer of the cooperative movement in India, Ramkrishna Lajmi, who was a pillar of strength to the cotton merchants N. Sirur & Co. and Raghunath K.Golikeri who later plunged into the nationalist movement.

After the demise of Shamrao Vithal in 1905, Talmaki took the lead and with the help of friends formed the Shamrao Vithal Cooperative Credit Society in 1907. Ganpat Kulkarni was one of the founders of this society. The society helped a large number of entrepreneurs at that time but it mostly attended to the temporary needs of its members on several occasions when funds were needed by them for domestic and personal reasons. Whether the Karnatak Press, now under Ganpat, received any financial assistance from the Society in its difficult period is not known. But some of the individual friends from those mentioned above must have certainly lent a little support. But presently we will allude to the two occasions when Karnatak Press and the Shamrao Vithal Cooperative Credit Society interacted in the circumstances and position that deserve to be noted as indicating a phase in the economic life of the people of those times. Both these occasions are after the passing away of Ganpat and when his younger brother Mangesh was at the helm.

It is really amazing that the Nadkarni brothers and later Ganpat Kulkarni, took up the ventures when they were comparatively young in age. Though we do not know how old were they when they were at the helm of these undertakings, we have some other data from which we can do some guesswork. Mangesh Kulkarni was born in 1887. We assume that Ganpat was the eldest son in the Kulkarni family. Ganpat perhaps was born around 1877, which indicates that he was hardly 22 or 23 when he made the bold offer to take over the press from the Nadkarnis. The Nadkarnis too probably started at a similar age, certainly less than 25, when they established the Karnatak Press. Let us also remember that they had hardly any formal education as we know of today. In fact at that time young people had migrated from their native places to towns as educational facilities or employment opportunities were not available to them. When they came to towns they took up jobs or some profession very

Ganpat Narayan Kulkarni
(? - 1918)

early in life. There are many instances when these young persons mentioned wrong birth dates for records, because they had not yet attained the minimum age stipulated for appointments in government service.

What these young people lacked in formal education they made up for by hard work and their ability to learn through harsh life and most important of all, they struggled to achieve success and had a desire to be of service to the society. It is true that there were opportunities too for those who were prepared to grab them. Added to these qualities was the daring to take risks when they took up professional or vocational work.

A word about the Girgaon area of Bombay will not be out of context. This area, in the last decades of the

Girgaon (late 19th century)

nineteenth century and early decades of the twentieth century, bears no resemblance whatsoever to the bustling traffic or chaos that we find there today. Of course, Bombay has changed and there has been tremendous growth in the density of population, various activities, business, education and social life. Nevertheless, even in those days, Girgaon was a hub of activity. It had the advantage of being close to the Fort area where the Government headquarters as well as British business establishments were located. On this Girgaon Road lived the legendary figure of the century – Nana Shankerset. It was also the main residential area of the Pathare Prabhu community who were among the earliest settlers of this island city. The population of the city was hardly 10 lakhs at the end of the nineteenth century and the city limits were up to the Mahim creek only*. However, the main urban activities were probably limited to the southern part or at the most to the central part of Bombay which was the industrial and textile belt.

Ganpat was an experienced press-worker. He was a type-setter in the Nadkarni regime. Perhaps he did not realize the heavy responsibilities of an entrepreneur when he thought of owning the Press himself. He moved the location from a by-lane to the main street of Thakurdwar. In any case he did not seem to have possessed the three major requirements of an entrepreneur – financial management, human resource development and public relations that made a good entrepreneur. We cannot say he was completely devoid of them but certainly he was found wanting in some measure.

P. B. Kulkarni, who has outlined sketches of many famous printers and publishers of the nineteenth and twentieth centuries in his book tracing the history of the Nirnay Sagar Press, has given some hints about this in his narrative. The information provided by him must be taken with some reservation as P. B. Kulkarni tends to be hyperbolic in his assessment of men and situations. He reports that Ganpat Kulkarni had incurred a debt of Rs. 40,000 at the time he handed over the management of Karnatak Press to his brother in about 1914. He also states that the annual turnover of the Press was about Rs. 60,000. As we have already noted, Ganpat was active in the social activities of the members of the Chitrapur Saraswat community and was one of the founders of the Shamrao Vithal Co-operative Credit Society. It is not

* Census of 1891 records the population of Bombay as 8.21 lakhs. It dwindled to 7.75 in 1901 census because of the plague epidemic.

possible for us to somehow accept that he could incur such huge debt within a decade of taking over the Press. We often find that even a good manager cannot be a mature and successful entrepreneur if he lacks the qualities we have mentioned above. We also know that Ganpat was troubled by ill-health for a long time, which must have restricted his ability to run the establishment successfully. In any case, one principle that every leader of industry has to keep in mind is that he should match expenses with revenue – he cannot have deficit financing year after year. Ganpat decided to take the help of his younger brother Mangesh when he found that things were getting out of his control. Mangesh did have some time to pick up the burden of the Printing Press before his brother succumbed to an illness in 1918.

5

1916-1945

If Ganpat was an enterprising person, his younger brother Mangesh was much more daring and adventurous. During his long life of over 80 years he took risks, achieved a lot, failed many times and suffered many misfortunes and hardships. There were trying times of personal grief and business losses which would have broken the weak. But he managed to keep his cool, all the time. One could describe him as a braveheart.

Mangesh was born in 1887 and died on 12 February 1968. Very little information could be gathered about his childhood days. Both, Ganpat, the elder brother and Mangesh must have spent their entire pre-teen days in Bankikodla till they came to Bombay for starting their careers. In those days facilities for education were meagre. Bankikodla had schools only for primary education up to the fourth standard. If anyone was eager to study further he had to go to faraway district towns. The other alternative available was the service offered by some well-read seniors who would volunteer to teach the students beyond primary school stage and also coach them in English so that they could face competition when they thought of taking up jobs at places away from the home-town. Perhaps the first High School established in Bankikodla was the one founded with the help of the Kulkarnis.

P. B. Kulkarni in his book *Nirnay Sagarachi Akshar Sadhana* has written a chapter on 'The Achievements of the Karnatak Printing Press'. He had an opportunity to meet Mangesh and the information given by him can be taken as authentic, though as we have already noted he had a tendency to glorify and exaggerate. He has stated that Mangesh had studied up to the fourth standard. In those days there was only one school called Anglo-Vernacular School in Bankikodla and Mangesh must have had his schooling there. He must have finished his primary school education when his elder brother concluded his talk with the Nadkarnis and decided to buy Karnatak sometime in 1896.

Mangesh joined his brother in or about 1912. He took complete charge of the Press in 1916. He had little knowledge about the details of the printing or publishing industry; but he was pragmatic and quickly grasped not only the fundamentals but also what was needed to make the press a full-fledged unit which could serve the needs of its customers. His earlier service in the two famous publishing houses – Longman, Green & Co. and Blackie & Sons (even if it was for short durations) must have given him some idea of the industry. He also had a genial temperament, pleasant manners and adventurous spirit. The First World War was still on when he took up the reins of the Press. Government propaganda literature was being printed in large quantities and it was a lucrative business. However, the authorities were inclined to channelise all the printing work to presses owned by the British. We do not have information about the persons whom he contacted and who were close to the 'buyers' of such material in the Government. But Mangesh did manage to get a good part of the printing work.

We also do not have records of when he thought of the Karnatak Type Foundry. Apparently, if business was growing he could not depend on outside type foundries, who were, in a way, his competitors. At that time Javji Dadaji Type Foundry cast types but the Nirnay Sagar Press owned by them had a formidable publication programme. Mangesh was one of the first to install an Inter-Type Machine which could increase the output considerably, though the hand-composing section remained a major part of his outfit for a long time. Because it often became necessary to combine the use of types by the processes of hand-composing and inter-type composing in printing, he encouraged his type casters to prepare moulds for all the English fonts that the Inter-Type machine used. For Devnagari he had his own types known as 'Karnatak' types including the 'akhand pica' one of the (as certified by expert Bapurao Naik) elegant, useful types in the printing industry of that period. Till the advent of Desk Top Publishing (DTP) elegant types cast by type foundries were in demand from smaller printers from all over Maharashtra. At that time only a few type foundries like Javji Dadaji Type Foundry, Gujarat Type Foundry, both from Bombay, and Jnanprakash Type Foundry from Pune had a variety of type fonts. Again we have no information whether Mangesh supplied types to other printers. (But we do know that after he sold the unit to Dhawales the type foundry was used only for its home productions.) Mangesh almost came up to the standards of Nirnay Sagar Press which by now had become world-renowned (particularly among scholars of Sanskrit literature.). Karnatak secured some of this business and also took over some business from the reputable British-

Mangesh Narayan Kulkarni
(1887 - 1968)

owned printers such as Times of India Press and Caxton Printing Press. What is surprising is that this was achieved in the shortest possible time. It has prompted the eminent scholar Bapurao Naik, who has written the most authentic, well-documented book in Marathi, *Bharatiya Granth Mudran*, to state that 1918 to 1945 be regarded as 'Karnatak Yug'. No mean compliment! Many other achievements in other fields were to follow.

Let us try to examine the different aspects of Mangesh's personality and approach to work. When Mangesh took interest in the management of the Press in 1912 he was about 29 years old. In the following years till 1918, when he became the sole owner of the establishment, after the demise of his brother, he must have picked up not only the minute details of press management, but also prepared his work plans. As we have noted earlier in the period 1902-1916, of which we have scanty knowledge, perhaps he was involved in many activities which gave him experience and introduced him to the ways of the world. For example, P. B. Kulkarni in his book referred to earlier, has stated that by 1916-1918 Mangesh had incurred a loss of six lakhs of rupees in his business of trading in cement in which he was engaged. The end of the World War I brought in recession and all the cement he had bought could not be sold and had to be stored in godowns only to attract a burden of rent. On the face of it the figure of six lakhs seems to be an exaggeration. But those who know Mangesh's venture-some dealings perhaps will find this statement in the realm of possibility. The different types of businesses he handled in his life lends further credence to the information provided by P. B. Kulkarni.

In this connection we have to take into account major

भाग दुसरा

नियतकालिकांचा इतिहास

(मासिकें – त्रैमासिकें – वगैरे)

मराठी पहिलीं नियतकालिकें

(१)

मराठींतील पहिलें वृत्तपत्र काढण्याचा मान ज्याप्रमाणें श्री. बाळशास्त्री जांभेकर व श्री. भाऊ महाजन यांच्याकडे जातो, त्याप्रमाणें मराठींतहि पहिलें नियतकालिक '**दिग्दर्शन**' १८३७त सुरू करण्याचा मानहि त्यांच्याकडेच जातो. मराठी नियतकालिक '**मराठी ज्ञानप्रसारक**' हें मुंबईच्या 'उपयुक्त ज्ञानप्रसारक' सभेच्या विद्यमानें १८५० पासून सुरू झालें. हें मासिक सुमारें १५।१६ वर्षें चाललें होतें. इंग्रजी भाषेंतील भारदस्त अशा '**क्वार्टर्ली**'च्या धर्तीवर या मासिकाची आंखणी करण्यांत आली होती. मराठींतील दुसरें विख्यात त्रैमासिक '**ज्ञानदर्शन**' हें १८५४ मध्यें सुप्रसिद्ध वृत्तपत्रकार श्री. भाऊ महाजन यांच्याच संपादकत्वाखालीं सुरू झालें. त्यांनीं यापूर्वीच '**दिग्दर्शन**' व '**उपदेश-चंद्रिका**' चालविली होती. ज्ञानदर्शन या त्रैमासिकाच्या जुलै महिन्यांत प्रसिद्ध झालेल्या पहिल्या अंकांत श्री. भाऊसाहेबांनीं जी प्रस्तावना लिहिली आहे तींत (विविधज्ञानविस्तार १९२६ मे, पृ. १८७) वर्णिलेली परिस्थिति आजच्या घटकेसहि तशीच कायम आहे. तीन-चार वर्षांतच त्यांना हा आंतबट्ट्याचा व्यवहार सोडून द्यावा लागला. तिसरें नांवाजलेलें मासिक 'शाळापत्रक' हें १८६१ मध्यें '**पुणें पाठशाळापत्रक**' या नांवानें प्रथम प्रसिद्ध झालें व तिसऱ्या वर्षाच्या ४ थ्या अंकापासून तें मराठी 'शाळापत्रक' ह्याच नांवानें प्रसिद्ध होत होतें. त्यानंतर सुप्रसिद्ध अशा विविधज्ञानविस्तार मासिकाचा जन्म १८६७ च्या जुलैंत झाला. सुदैवानें गेलीं ६९ वर्षें विविधज्ञानविस्तार चालू असून विस्तारानें कित्येक लेखकांना आणि कवींना लेखन-प्रवण केलें आहे. विस्तारापूर्वीं लहान मोठीं किरकोळ २९ मासिकें निघालीं होतीं अशी नोंद सांपडते. '**न्यायाश्रय**' (१८६६) व '**वकिलांची साथी**' १८६७ हीं दोन कायद्याचींच मासिकें होतीं. त्याशिवाय '**ज्ञानोदय**' (१८४२), हरी केशवजी यांचें '**तारप्रसारक**' (१८५०), '**प्रभोदय**' (१८५६) व '**सायंदीपिका**' (जुनी) १८६१ हीं ख्रिस्तीमतप्रचारक मासिकें होतीं. '**विचारलहरी**' (१८५२), '**चंद्रिका**' (१८५४) व सद्धर्मदीपिका (१८५६) हीं तिन्ही मासिकें हिंदुधर्माचा प्रसार करून ख्रिस्तीमतप्रचाराला विरोध करीत होतीं.

आकृती ३६ : 'कर्नाटक'च्या अखंड पायक्यात जुळविलेले एक पान, 'नियतकालिकांचा इतिहास' कर्नाटक प्रेस, मुंबई

'Akhand Pica' Type
A Karnatak Type Foundry Innovation

aspects of his personality. He had the knack of befriending persons who could be of some help to him in someway or the other. He was shrewd enough to know that they need not be persons in high society or wealthy; but they had to be resourceful. They were those who had a circle of friends of their own so that when in need they could give the desired assistance.

Amongst those there were people in the Deccan Machinery Company and D. M. Mistry who gave him support almost till the end of his life. We have no details whether they were officially partners of Mangesh in some of his businesses. But we do know that they were his trustworthy companions. He had deposited with Deccan Machinery Company some of his funds. With D. M. Mistry it was much more. It appears that he was his business partner in film distribution. Mangesh and Mistry imported B-grade Hollywood films quite popular with the crowd and arranged to exhibit them in theatres in the mill area of Bombay. Mistry not only stood by him through thick and thin but even after Mangesh's demise he looked after his grand-daughter, a homoeopath, who was stricken by paralysis at a young age. The famous Gandhi biographer D. G. Tendulkar was another person who often visited Karnatak. He first came in contact with Mangesh when his *30 Months in Russia* in Marathi was printed and published by Karnatak. Later *Gandhiji* edited by him and Vithaldas Jhaveri was printed at Karnatak. When D. G. Tendulkar wanted funds for his eight-volume biography *Mahatma* to be printed at the Times of India Press (because by then he wanted help of Ramesh Sanzagiri, the chief of the art department of the Times of India Press in the production of the book), Mangesh gave Rs. 5000 to the project. Later on, when Mangesh was in need of funds and wanted to dispose off his property in Ballard Estate area he approached D. G. Tendulkar. This property was occupied by offices attached to the Indian Navy and it was not possible to get vacant possession of the premises. Mangesh used the good offices of Tendulkar to get the Government of India to buy the building. Tendulkar was close to Prime Minister Jawaharlal Nehru and was editing Nehru's letters to Indira at that time.

There was another person, almost a "mystery man", K. Krishnamurthy, an adventurer himself, of Bangalore, who was Mangesh's partner in many ventures. But this is a story that needs to be told in some detail. Krishnamurthy was a flamboyant young bachelor who was in import and export business during World War II. Mangesh, who was equally dashing (though no longer young; now, in his sixties) joined him in some of these transactions. How many we do not know. The person who introduced Krishnamurthy to Mangesh was a middleman, a commission agent, N. M. Sirur. Sirur was earlier an agent to procure cotton for the leading ginning mills in and around Bellary, a prosperous cotton district of Karnataka. He had shifted to Bangalore in the late thirties and during World War II. He was mostly acting as an insurance agent and also as a professional astrologer, an advisor to several businessmen. Krishnamurthy was one of his clients. I met Krishnamurthy in Bangalore sometime in the mid-1940s. I was entrusted by my father with an important assignment to recover a small amount from Krishnamurthy. (I do not remember the exact amount but it may have been Rs. 30,000.) It was an unusual transaction. Mangesh owed this amount to my father. He also had to receive the same amount from

Krishnamurthy; so the debt was swapped so to say. I was still an undergraduate then and it was one of my periodic travel jaunts. I met N. M. Sirur who summoned Krishnamurthy and they had a lengthy discussion. There was one more complication in this transaction. Krishnamurthy had sort of given Bhatkal a security of a flat in a building just opposite the Cricket Club of India, in the Fort area of Bombay, which was in the name of his mother. At that point of time we were interested in securing a flat and were looking out for a place of residence for my father whose health was not in good shape and this spacious apartment near the Marine Drive and with the facility of lifts would have suited him well. Sirur initially tried all his power of persuasion but could not make any headway. He also suggested that the Rolls Royce car that Krishnamurthy owned, which he rarely used and was lying in a rented garage, be disposed off, so that the debt could be paid. Krishnamurthy did not budge. (Perhaps this car too was pledged by him to some lender.) However, Sirur had a last arrow in his bow. He also knew the stubborn Krisnamurthy extremely well. Sirur was a party as a commission agent in many of the transactions Krishnamurthy had done during the war years, and he had records of these. Most importantly, he knew of the black money that was involved in these deals. He threatened to submit this information to the Income Tax Department with the inevitable consequence. After a few minutes Krishnamurthy relented. It was a dangerous ultimatum for him and soon he settled the matter, though he did manage to get some extension of time from my gentle, gullible father. We lost the spacious apartment but got back the money – though without interest!

It was from this negotiation that I learnt that Mangesh

and Krishnamurthy had several dealings. At least two of them I remember. They had imported for some of the wealthy landlords of Madras Presidency, a couple of small aeroplanes. Another was the import of many heavy-duty farm tractors from Russia costing a whopping Rs. 25,000. This was more than the price of Ford Motors' cars which were also then available for half the price. They had to make distress sale of their stocks and they lost a good deal in this enterprise as well. It was part of business. They enjoyed it and perhaps would have been unhappy without such setbacks! We got to know only about the unsuccessful ones; perhaps they had many others in which they made profits.

My father G. R. Bhatkal was one of his trusted companions. (Later on I too had the privilege of enjoying Mangesh's trust and confidence.) He had worked with young G. R. Bhatkal when for a few months he worked at Karnatak after Matriculation in 1918. Mangesh was possibly one of those who encouraged Bhatkal to start Popular Book Depot. At this time, he must have recommended his relative Narsing Venkatesh Kulkarni of Dharwar to approach Ganpat Bhatkal for an alliance for his daughter Mitrabai (my mother). The Bhatkals also helped Mangesh to tide over many financial needs when he borrowed from 'the hundi market'. This is a complicated financial procedure which we will elaborate when we come to the difficult times that Mangesh's successors the Dhawales faced, as I was personally involved in the settlement of these transactions in the year 1960-61 as a co-lessee of Karnatak.

He probably had many other well-wishers and some business partners too, not known to us but those who helped him in his career, not directly in his business. So far as his business was concerned he had from the outset followed a management policy or style that enabled him to concentrate more on financial management, business development, plant expansion (as and when needed), updating equipment, developing new type fonts etc. He had, therefore, enough time to devote to his other ventures too about which we have got a glimpse already. In the management of the press he believed in delegation of duties. For the Marathi department he had as manager Bhau Puranik and for the English department Ganesh Mallapur both of whom enjoyed his full trust. It is said that the Oxford University Press used to offer a guinea as a prize to anyone who could detect a spelling error in their publications. Perhaps the same standards can be said to be true about Karnatak Press. Of course, in those days proof-reading was done meticulously by most of the printing plants and particular attention was paid to this aspect of production of books or journals. Later, when Karnatak's publication department expanded, the need for a competent editor was felt. Gangadhar Deorao Khanolkar seems to have performed this role for some time.

In an obituary note in the *Kanara Saraswat* we find reference to Mangesh's service with prominent publishers of the time, Longman, Green and Co. and Blackie and Sons. Chitrapur Saraswats did not find it difficult to obtain employment in the Government departments or in private enterprises. They had more than average proficiency in English language. They were known for their integrity and preferred to serve in the knowledge industry. Thus many who came to Bombay did find jobs in the British publishing firms. Some amongst them at some time or the other served in these establishments and made a mark for themselves in similar fields in the last century. Some names that come to mind are : B K Kumble, who was in charge of the London office of the Asia Publishing House, India's leading post-war publishing house (publishing a book a day in its heyday); Anand Kundaji who started with International Book House and later was founder-manager of Wiley Eastern Pvt. Ltd. (now known as New Age Publishers); S. R. Nirody, sometime stores in-charge at Oxford University Press, Bombay and later book promotion wizard at Popular Book Depot, Shanta Ram Rao of Orient Longman; Basrur Mangesh the leading supplier to educational institutions, K. Krishnamurthy of Chennai; P R Kaikini, a poet, who for many years was with the Publications Division, Government of India, in the Complete Works of Mahatma Gandhi project; G. D. Sthalekar at Orient Longman; apart from some authors like Girish Karnad (sometime with Oxford University Press) and Radha Kodange with Orient Longman. In journalism there were Mangesh Nadkarni (the co-founder of Karnatak), D. R. Mankekar, Sudhakar Bhat, U. Bhaskar Rao, S. R. Kolpe and several others.

In the development of the Karnatak Publishing House, the first name that comes to our mind is that of Prabhakar Shripat Bhase (? – 1925), the founder of *Bharat Gaurav Granthmala*. This was started by Bhase with a couple of books written by himself titled *Samaj Kantak* or *Venu*, one of which was printed at Karnatak. Starting with the three books published in 1911, most of the publications in this series (the series till 1939 had a total of 138 publications) were printed in the Karnatak Printing Press. Perhaps because of the pressure of work at the Karnatak Printing Press, a few got printed elsewhere. The series was taken over by Mangesh in 1925 after Bhase's demise. In those days there were many such serial publications which were popular. But the important and distinctive feature of *Bharat Gaurav Granthmala* was that it had a variety of subjects – fiction, biography, political analysis, religion, philosophy, and even poetry. Most of the other serial publications (*malas*) catered to popular taste, namely fiction and religious subjects. The very object of *Bharat Gaurav Granthmala* was to raise the level of the reading public to a higher plane. We therefore find in this list names of authors who became leading figures of Marathi literature – V. S. Khandekar, V. S. Gurjar, G. D. Madkholkar, poet B. B. Borkar, N. K. Behere, M. D. Altekar, Prabhakar Padhye, S. R. Tikekar, Vishnu Laxman Bhave, Bharat Ratna P. V. Kane, Shridhar Vyankatesh Ketkar (his milestone play was *Brahmankanya*), Bhargavram (Mama) Warerkar, J. R. Ajgaonker, Shankar Oak and Kumudini Prabhavalkar. Prabhakar Bhase was himself a prolific writer.

Even in the *Bharat Gaurav Granthmala* he has authored scores of books, while a few others written by him were published by other publishers. Translation of the entire works of Bankim Chandra Chatterji were made available to Marathi readers due to him. All the books in the series were lucidly written, and were in simple language and appealing in narration. (Though Mangesh, the publisher, always appealed to readers for greater support for the series and periodically threatened that it may have to be closed down due to lack of enough subscribers it continued to be published till 1939, when Mangesh turned his attention to textbooks for schools and colleges. Dhawale reprinted many titles from this series and also added some more titles – even after he had sold the printing plant in 1963).

Bankim Chandra, through his novels, depicted the life of the Bengali society of his time. He was also known for his nationalistic views and had contributed to the national movement. His song "Vande Mataram" in the novel *Anand Math* has been dear to people of all political opinions and has wide national acclaim. Bhase and Mangesh wanted to make their own contribution by making Bankim Babu's novels available in Maharashtra.

There were several other ways in which Mangesh was to serve the national freedom movement; but we will have occasion to note these a little later.

Mangesh was fearless, undaunted and had an unusual ability to handle difficult and knotty situations. His passion for public relations (which we have earlier mentioned) enabled him to face anyone, whatever be the position or status he enjoyed in the society or whatever authority he wielded. These abilities were evident in ample measure during the World War II. Even earlier the British Government was vigilant about public opinion and any literature that was published against the Government and which favoured the national movement was monitored and controlled, especially after the passing of the Press and Registration of Books Act (1867). We have evidence of the "Annual Report of Native Publications" from which we have some documentation about the *Kannada Suvarte* which was printed and published by Karnatak Press in the nineteenth century. Mangesh's foray in the field of journalism was perhaps by accident or because of his inner desire to encourage young, enterprising, dashing individuals. One such individual was Gangadhar Devrao Khanolkar.

6

G. D. Khanolkar

Gangadhar Devrao Khanolkar (1903-92) was a man of many parts. During his long life he chose service to literature as his sole goal. Born in a family of modest means in a village near the southernmost part of Maharashtra, his early childhood was a journey through several places because of his father's transferable jobs. Though he was adopted by his uncle, he was always looked after by his father, who in his later life became a 'Fakir'. Actually, if his father had his way Gangadhar would also have become the head of a small religious family math at Golvan.

But this little boy had other visions. Already his father, a well-read person, had inculcated in him an urge for the acquisition of knowledge. Added to this was his own innate desire and urge to learn languages, to respect the strength and power of words, love for literature in general, and lust for knowledge. This was backed by the influences at the school, by his contemporaries and his elder brother. Others who influenced Khanolkar and with whom he interacted continuously later became notable figures in the literary world. When he passed matriculation he thought of going to Shantiniketan where for nearly two years he had liberal education under the aegis of Gurudev Rabindranath Tagore himself. This

G. D. Khanolkar
(1903-1992)

institution was started by the poet in 1901 and already it was known for being a centre of the gurukul system of education – the poet's vision, version and dream. Shantiniketan (Abode of Peace) was started by Gurudev Tagore on 22 December 1901 as a school. Later on when the poet received the Noble Prize for literature, it was upgraded to an institution for higher learning in 1913. It received official status of a University after Independence and was renamed Vishva Bharati (India International) in 1951. After returning from Shantiniketan, Khanolkar took up some teaching jobs; but then plunged headlong into achieving the goal he had set for himself – service through literature.

Khanolkar's first book was a biography of his literary guru, Shripad Krishna Kolhatkar. This was in 1926 and the book was printed and published by Karnatak. Thus Khanolkar was associated with Karnatak and its successive owners in some form or another all through his life. For over six decades he was a trusted, faithful part of Karnatak, devoted to the organization and the families that controlled its destinies. By any standards he was an independent-minded personality. Stocky in physique, his exterior gave an impression that he did not seem to savour close friendship. However, there were two very important traits that distinguished him from others. He was hardworking, and he concentrated deeply on whatever assignment or project he was engaged in, rarely bothered by what was going on around. Perhaps a contradiction, but he did have his ears tuned to the conversations of others. He was a voracious reader and a prolific writer. Educated at Gurudev Rabindranath's Shantiniketan he had a broad outlook on life. Apart from his unattractive build and his often rough way of talking, he was a man of versatile talent.

A friend of many eminent literary luminaries of the time, his forte was research. Editing in the true sense of the word was also a pastime. He spent many years of hard work on biographical tomes. That brought him the assignment of editing the 'Marathi Wangmay Kosha' which he had unfortunately to leave midway. However, the data he collected and also the several biographies he wrote are recognized as standard works – authentic and comprehensive reference material for scholars even today.

When Khanolkar came to Mangesh of Karnatak as an author in 1926, Mangesh had already obtained the ownership of the *Bharat Gaurav Granthmala* and wanted someone as an advisor and as an editor in the publication house. Khanolkar had developed contacts with a group of writers who were to make substantial contribution to Marathi literature. Many of the writers who wrote for the *Bharat Gaurav Granthmala* must have been introduced to Mangesh by Khanolkar. From 1926-92 Khanolkar was associated with Karnatak in various capacities.

This over six decades of long association was more in the nature of two individuals, dedicated to serve the printed word, bonded by personal affection rather than any monetary considerations. For Khanolkar it was first Mangesh Kulkarni; later after 1945, Balkrishna Ganesh Dhawale and after him his son Dhananjay Dhawale. All of them treated him as a trustworthy associate in their various projects.

Off and on, Khanolkar did indulge in his favourite, shall we say, passion through involvement in many directions.

He co-edited *Pragati* (1926-29), started his own *Pratibha* (1932-33). He was associated with another literary monthly *Jyotsna* (1936).

He worked assiduously on his multi-volume *Arvachin Marathi Wangmay Sevak*. Later he also edited the first volume of the *Marathi Wangmay Kosha* (950 A.D. to 1850 A. D.).

He wrote biographies of his literary guru Shripad Krishna Kolhatkar, Vishnu Govind Vijapurkar, Rabindranath Tagore, Walchand Hirachand and Madhav Julian. A few of these were published by Karnatak.

He edited a number of memorial volumes. *Keshav Bhikaji Dhawale* (1950), *Sonyache Divas* (1974), *Trimbak Shankar Shejwalkar* (1977), *Dhananjay Keer* (1979), *Vishrabdh Sharada* Vol II, letters written by literary figures and Sridhar Vyankatesh Ketkar's *Wangmay Vishayatale Lekha* (1975).

For Karnatak he co-edited textbooks: *Maharashtra Sahitya Parichay, Gadya Vaibhav* and *Maharashtra Rasavanti* (three parts each).

For some time, he was managing Bombay Book Depot (1946-47). In 1938 he started a publishing firm, Swastik Publishing Company.

At the time of his death in 1992, he had almost completed the manuscripts of the revised edition of *Arvachin Marathi Wangmay Sevak*, an unfinished biography of Swami Vivekanand and copious notes on the Mahanubhav sect which has a noticeable presence in Maharashtra and a major part of the *Marathi Wangmay Kosha*.

From 1973 to 1985 he worked on the second part of the New Standard Dictionary. This was an unfinished work started for Keshav Bhikaji Dhawale by S. R. Sirmukadam, who had done work on the letters A to N and the printed forms were stacked up in sheets for many years. When the third generation boss of Dhawale approached him for help he readily agreed to complete the formidable work. When Dhananjay Dhawale inquired about the remuneration that he expected, his reply was typical of the person. "I will be doing this not for money but for my love for the institution for which I have worked for decades."

Khanolkar never bothered about monetary returns or rewards in any other form. He was honoured by Marathi Sahitya Parishad, Pune (1988), Konkan Marathi Sahitya Parishad (1990) and Venus Prakashan, Pune (1991). He was also felicitated on his 75th birthday.

7

Mangesh Kulkarni

Mangesh's brother Ganpat was keeping indifferent health and so Mangesh started assisting his brother at 'Karnatak' around 1916 and took over complete charge of the Press in 1918 after his brother's demise. He handed over the flourishing Press to the Dhawales in 1945.

Mangesh's career in the brief span of about three decades of Karnatak Press under him, can be divided into three phases. In the first phase till about 1925, his efforts were concentrated on the development of the press, its expansion, and setting up of the type foundry etc. Mangesh was also able to get some printing jobs so far given exclusively to printing presses owned by Britishers, such as Times of India Press, Caxton Printing Press, Onlooker Press and others. This coincided with the taking over of the entire responsibility of the *Bharat Gaurav Granthmala*, after the death of its founder, Prabhakar Bhase. During the second phase from 1926 to 1932 or more precisely till 1935, when Karnatak was shifted to Chira Bazar, there was a spurt in publishing activities and we can say that both printing and publishing were receiving equal attention. After 1935, the third phase began with the publishing of a number of textbooks in the late thirties which was a greater responsibility of preparing and promoting educational books.

Karnatak House (Chira Bazar)

As the business expanded and got more organized the need for a more sizeable and prominent place was felt. It is not possible to trace all the sites and locations where "Karnatak" was located ever since it was started way back in the closing decades of eighteenth century. From available records we have been able to note the following:

1893 : *Kannada Suvarte*, mentions Karnatak Press but does not give the address.

1919 : *Kanara Saraswat*, a quarterly was printed by Karnatak Printing Press at Haji Cussume Building, Thakurdwar, Post Kalabadevi.

1927 : *Kanara Saraswat*, the address recorded in the

same magazine was 318 A Thakurdwar.

1935 : Shifted to its own premises at Chira Bazar.

An interesting feature of those times is the form of names of the establishments. In academic parlance we know of a proprietary concern, partnership or a company (which is governed under the Companies Act with limited liability of shareholders). But perhaps following the style of some of the British establishments many Indian proprietary concerns styled themselves "XYZ and Co". For example, Macmillan & Co., Bennett Coleman & Co. were known and well-established in Bombay. We have a record of M. N. Kulkarni & Co., Stationers, as address of M. N. Kulkarni in the membership list of The Kanara Saraswat Association, in 1912. It is also possible that this was formed to supply paper and printing material to the press or the enterprising Mangesh really had a go in this activity too!

But a more interesting and significant event in this connection appears in 1920 after Mangesh became the sole proprietor of Karnatak Printing Press. In that year G. N. Kulkarni & Co. was formed. It appears that the bankers, Shamrao Vithal Cooperative Credit Society (now the Shamrao Vithal Cooperative Bank) could not give a loan of more than Rs. 5000 to an individual borrower. Apparently those who needed more funds had to make alternative arrangements. One way was for a group of individuals to come together and form a company and thus G. N. Kulkarni & Co. was established. It had a short life – perhaps just one general body meeting. What is interesting is that many of those individuals who were its members were office-bearers of the Bank. We have already noted that Ganpat, Mangesh's brother, was one of the founders of the Shamrao Vithal Cooperative

Credit Society formed in 1907.

After Mangesh had a complete hold of the business and specially after his becoming the sole proprietor of the prestigious *Bharat Gaurav Granthmala* after the demise of Prabhakar Bhase in 1925, he got interested in some more exciting projects. We do not know whether he had planned these projects himself or they just came to him. It was also the time of the important phase of the freedom movement under the leadership of Mahatma Gandhi. The Government on its part was alert and kept a special watch on printing presses. One of the authors who wrote for *Bharat Gaurav Granthmala* was the renowned historian, Govind Sakharam Sardesai (1865 to 1959). His multi-volume History of India from 1000-1848 in Marathi was published as 'Musalmani Riyasat', 'Marathi Riyasat' and 'British Riyasat'. It is an extremely well-documented standard reference work used by students and scholars alike even today. Trimbak Shankar Shejwalkar (1895-1963), a student of history was assisting Sardesai on some of the projects. Shejwalkar, in 1916 just out of his teens, was keen on studying war strategies and related data. For this purpose he wanted to join the army during World War I. Disqualified because he could not fit into the norms set for recruits he joined the war department's recruitment office. It seems he had a one-sided infatuation for a girl working as a colleague in that office. Jilted by her, he was a disappointed soul. He immersed himself in studies of all subjects related to wars, its history etc. He spent most of his time at the Royal Asiatic Society Library and with Sardesai, and possibly also at the Karnatak Printing Press, who were publishers of Sardesai's books. The battles of Panipat have fascinated historians and different views have been propounded about the strategies of the warring armies at this site. Mangesh suggested to Sardesai that a popular version of the battle be written for *Bharat Gaurav Granthmala*. Sardesai in turn gave this assignment to Shejwalkar who was working with him and asked him to prepare a manuscript from the material already available in the 'Marathi Riyasat'. Shejwalkar worked on this assiduously, prepared the manuscript expeditiously and competently. This was published in 1926 as *Balaji Bajirao Nanasaheb Peshave*. While preparing the manuscript, however, Shejwalkar was discussing the subject with his senior and he vehemently argued against some views expressed in the thesis. It was Sardesai's turn to surprise his student. He asked Shejwalkar to write on his own judgment on the subject and requested the publishers to include his views as a Foreword to the book. Indeed a rare example of a reputed scholar recognizing the merit of a budding scholar, thirty years his junior.

Shejwalkar had many upsets in his life and at a particular point in his career in his early twenties, he was very much depressed and even thought of ending his life. At this juncture some of his friends, more particularly Khanolkar who was helping Mangesh as editor in the publishing department, suggested that Shejwalkar may be given an opportunity to venture into some constructive activity. And thus was born the weekly *Pragati* (8 June 1929 to 11 February 1932).

Reminiscent of *Kannada Suvarate,* the periodical printed and published at Karnatak Press in the earlier century, the weekly in Marathi, *Pragati,* also, during its short life, played the role of a chronicle and an outspoken commentator on the social, economic and political events of that period. Of course, some of the editorial views brought down the wrath of the authorities and Mangesh had to face them with explanations and often he had to keep large sums as security deposit. Ultimately the journal had to succumb to the unbearable demand of a deposit of Rs. 10,000. Mangesh by sponsoring this periodical saved the life of Shejwalkar, the budding, sincere, genius-like historian.

Mangesh contributed to the freedom struggle in his own way. He also knew that he had the press workers to keep in mind whose livelihood was dependent on the job. Thus, while he did print a lot of material which was considered seditious by the Government, once he found that it would jeopardize the interest of the press, he got the material printed by a small printer assuring him that he would be compensated for any loss if the Government did take action against him. He even assured him that his family would be looked after during the period of his incarceration if that happened. He kept his word when such an occasion did arise.

There is an interesting episode worth mentioning in connection with his dealing with such matters. We have already noted earlier that he was a seasoned public relations man. He had kept his contacts with everyone who he thought could protect his interests. He had friendly relations with officers in all departments of the Government which had some connection with his industry. Mr. Maxwell, Secretary of the Home Department was one such officer with whom Mangesh had cordial relations. Karnatak had deposited Rs. 10,000 as security with the department. Once, when possibly he was in dire need of money he approached Mr. Maxwell and requested him to make the amount available to him. Mr. Maxwell's advice was that of a real friend. He told Mangesh, "You are very often found guilty of publishing literature which my department finds objectionable. I can refund the deposit to you as per your request. But it is possible that the Government may ask you for larger amounts later. At present you are in safe hands as long as I am in this position."Apparently Mangesh had the knack of keeping his benefactors satisfied!.

Karnatak used to publish *The New Indian Antiquary* (1938-1947), a prestigious periodical in which orientalists, indologists and historians from India and abroad contributed articles. This journal is considered as a valuable reference magazine by scholars even today.

The major contribution of Mangesh can be said to be in the field of producing and publishing of textbooks for schools. In the early thirties he thought of producing graded language readers for students from the pre-primary to the high school level. Once an idea occurred to him, it became an obsession with him and he would look out for the most competent person who could undertake the project. Prahlad Keshav Atre had already gained some reputation in educational circles. He had just returned to India after obtaining a Teacher's Diploma in London. He had his own dreams about improving the standard of textbooks which so far were dominated by literature selected by the people who owed allegiance to the Emperor George V, whose sketch appeared on the cover of the textbooks. Thus two dreamers Mangesh Kulkarni and P. K. Atre produced *Navyug Wachan Mala* in Marathi, the first series that broke the monopoly of Government-sponsored educational literature. Atre had a thorough grasp of the subject. Mangesh knew his worth. In their first meeting itself Atre told him that preparing

Government Series

Karnatak Series

textbooks of this type was a good idea; but it involved considerable expenses. Atre thought that he could put off the publisher and mentioned a high figure of five to six thousand rupees as preliminary expenses. Mangesh paid him Rs. 6000 immediately. And thus began the journey of publishing of textbooks at primary, middle and high school level. The experiment was repeated in Gujarati too. To ensure the success of the publication, Mangesh persuaded Atre to have as a co-author, a non-Brahmin Vithalrao Ghate. In those days this pattern of a Brahmin-non-Brahmin co-authored books became a necessity for a publisher.

The series was such a success that Atre writes in his autobiography that while his pay as a teacher was Rs. 75 per month, he spent Rs. 200 per month for petrol for his new blue Landmark Chevrolet car. This instance is indicative of how Karnatak authors prospered. So also the institution gained considerable financial success.

Textbook publishing, however, was to last for just about a decade. Mangesh's personal life was no bed of roses. In the early 1940s, he had to face calamities that he could hardly bear. Whatever be the severity of business difficulties and financial worries, he could handle them with a brave heart. But this time it was something he could not bear and thus succumbed to its pressure. He lost his wife, daughter and his only son within a very short period of time. Mangesh lost all hopes of any one from his family being available to keep him in the business. The old guard assisting him were getting superannuated. He could not recruit new talent. So in desperation he thought of concentrating on the few other sources of his income (like returns on deposits, film distribution etc.) and encash the major asset of the Karnatak by selling it at a reasonable price. Some of his friends in the community tried to bid, but their offer – even as it was in a consortium - could not match the figure that was offered by Keshav Bhikaji Dhawale, another reputed institution in Maharashtra in the field of publishing.

Even towards the end of his life he rarely showed despair or fatigue on his face. He travelled by public transport everyday, attended to his routine 'diabetic' life, administering the daily dose of insulin himself.

Risky business was his hobby, philanthropy his obsession. Post Karnatak, his woes continued. His daughter-in-law had bouts of mental depression and his son's daughter, a homoeopath, became stone deaf. He continued to give them support.

Mangesh, of course, continued his activities in other fields: film distribution, trading etc. But his old vision was not seen thereafter. His philanthropic activities continued. He spent some time on the development of the Laxmi Narayan Mandir (temple) he had built in his hometown, Bankikodla. When he breathed his last on 12 February 1968, he had spent a day of normal activity. He left to his successors a fraction of the wealth he had earned during his lifetime.

8

Sonyabapu Dhawale

Keshav Bhikaji Dhawale, a family firm, took over Karnatak on 19 September 1945. The amount they paid for the unit was at least 20 per cent more than a fair value of the assets. There were many considerations that must have weighed in the mind of B.G. Dhawale, the supremo of the publishing firm. We will refer to him as "Sonyabapu" as he was popularly known.

In the last few years they were getting the printing work done by a couple of printing presses which gave reasonably good work, to the norms set by Dhawale. But the schedules were not completely in their control. Besides, Sonyabapu must have felt that he would get full scope for his talents in the production of literature if he owned a unit of the dimension that Karnatak was at that time.

There was another relevant factor encouraging his decision. The "Selection of Marathi Literature" and "Sanskrit Veche", selection for the matriculation examination were being assigned to one among three bidders for printing and distributing. It was considered an assured and a sizeable market by any publisher as it also gave the publisher an advantage in marketing his other publications. The three bidders were Nirnay Sagar Press, Karnatak Publishing House and Keshav Bhikaji Dhawale.

Nirnay Sagar was not a major player as their interests were primarily in Sanskrit publications. So, by buying Karnatak, Dhawales could eliminate competition and have monopoly in an important sector.

Whatever may be the compulsions Sonyabapu must have been thrilled by the very sight of this unit which was what may be called not only full-fledged but also with a huge potential for expansion.

If Mangesh was a pioneer of sorts, Sonyabapu was a dreamer *par excellence*. Before we proceed further with the history of the progress from 1945 to 1963 when the Karnatak building was sold by Sonyabapu it will be interesting to trace briefly the background of Sonyabapu and Keshav Bhikaji Dhawale.

"Keshav Bhikaji Dhawale", as per the official records, was founded on Ganesh Chaturthi day in Madhavbagh, then a hub of book selling activity, very near the Mumbadevi temple, in Bombay. It was founded by the brothers – Mahadev (1873 to March 1910), Keshav (5-7-1882 to 1-12-1957) and Ganesh (21-7-1888 to 15-5-1938). They belonged to an orthodox Karhade Brahman family. The Dhawales started their career as teachers. They had started a school at Bhoiwada in the Parel area of Bombay city. Mahadev was earning Rs. 7 per month as a teacher in the village Shipoli in the Ratnagiri District of the Bombay Presidency. This was during the turn of the nineteenth century. The city was affected by plague and they could not run the Parel school to get enough money to maintain themselves. The next occupation they chose was the business of selling books. With a borrowed capital of Rs. 200 they bought books that were in popular demand such as sthotras, primer of alphabets and numbers, bhajans, etc. and set up a make-shift stall on an open katta

Sonyabapu Dhawale
(1915 - 1973)

Ganesh Bhikaji Dhawale
(1888 - 1938)

(parapet) under a peepal tree. Later they acquired a small shop in the same area. Strong believers in astrology, they named their firm, 'Keshav Bhikaji Dhawale', though he was the second brother among the three, because their astrologer had predicted that Keshav would bring them luck. Keshav had the longest life; the two others had comparatively shorter lives. But he could hardly contribute to the daily routine of the business as he was affected by several ailments throughout his life and later he almost had to restrict his movements to an armchair. Mahadev expired in 1910. Ganesh took over the management of the business. In 1914 they published their first book, "Little Book of Numbers" which was an instant success. In 1933, Ganesh also became a victim of serious ailments and

Keshav Bhikaji Dhawale (1882 - 1957)

succumbed to them in 1938.

Born on 15 May 1915 Sonyabapu was the only male member in the family. He had his schooling in Akshi where he was staying with his uncle Keshav. He later moved to Bombay and even joined the Elphinstone College for further studies.

Sonyabapu had to give up college education and join the business when his father, Ganesh, was unable to attend to it. He was 18 years of age then. The next 40 years of his life present a very interesting story of successes and failures. Sonyabapu with whom the present writer had the privilege of working made a fascinating study of a person – a student ready to learn and a perfectionist. Aptly described by his colleague G. D. Khanolkar :

Balkrishna Ganesh Dhawale was a personality full of contradictions. He denied to himself many essentials (kept his needs to the minimum). But on occasions he was extremely indulgent. He could be possessive; at the same time he did realise the importance of the core of Indian philosophy, being detached. Generally mild mannered, he could at times be caustic, even cantankerous. Soft and persuasive in speech, often he was unreasonably harsh to. He was equally successful in making friends. He could exhibit extreme patience. But several times he let out uncontrolled anger, inviting displeasure even to the extent of animosity. By nature he was a creative artist, and yet on rare occasions he shattered to pieces his own creations. He was a rare mixture of commendable merits and unbridled idealism.

As noted above he was the only male member in the family and thus a successor to the successful Dhawale firm. Even as a child he exhibited boisterous temperament which often embarrassed the members of the family, his teachers and well-wishers. Probably because he was a pampered child his temperamental traits continued even after 1933 when he assumed the responsibility of running the business. Except during the five years from 1933 to 1938, when we may assume he also acted as an apprentice to his father, he had his way in everything he wanted to do, fully blessed by his invalid uncle, Keshav, who hardly interfered in the business. This further steeled his inherent characteristic trait to take independent decisions and follow them with determination and boldness unmindful of their consequences. Financial considerations or the impact of his decisions on others did not bother him at all. It was not that he was an autocrat in any sense. He did value company; in fact he thrived in the company of friends. He also tried to learn from others, from their experience. He read books and all the literature that was relevant to his needs. At the height of his career he had a dozen colleagues working with him – all stalwarts in their own fields of expertise :

Khanolkar has in his biographical note divided Sonyabapu's professional career thus :

1939-45 : Years of apprentice up to the acquisition of the Karnatak

1946-1950 : Shifting the Press to Sion

1951-1957 : Awards and unexpected difficulties and demise of uncle Keshav

1958-1966 : Nandi Books, lease to Bhatkal and Chaudhari, Karnatak and Dhawale separated

1967-1973 : Post sale of Karnatak.

If the records of the earlier period of 1938–45 were available and studied they could present Sonyabapu as an efficient administrator, astute businessman and an enlightened and good publisher. The Dhawale firm had given up the main bookselling activity and had concentrated on publishing after 1915. *Mulinche Chimukale Pustak* was their first publication. They started publishing 'panchangs' (astrological almanacs) from 1924 and the famous Shree Samarth *rojnishi* from 1961. These annuals brought them a wide market. However their main list contained popular religious scriptures and philosophical works. Before Sonyabapu took over the management, Dhawales had shifted their business premises several times and in 1934 they shifted to their own building "Shree Samarth Sadan" in Benham Hall Lane, a crowded street in South Bombay. N.L.Chaudhari, the contractor who supervised the work of constructing the building, became a family friend and took up a role later that helped the firm to face a difficult situation in 1960. Till 1938, we find that Keshav Bhikaji Dhawale firm had cashed in on the trend in the general reading public of buying religious books – an experience that they had gained as booksellers – so much so that they even bought in 1924 the publication rights of "Eknathi Bhagwat" a famous Marathi commentary by saint-poet Eknath (1548-99) on a portion of the Sanskrit scriptural text *Bhagawatam* and some other books from Raoji Shridhar, titles which are selling in large numbers even today.

When Sonyabapu entered the business, he thought of another area of publishing, namely, children's books, which he considered would be a good addition to their list. During the 1930s and 1940s, most of the leading Marathi publishers of that time were already publishing children's books. These books were, in fact, published in the form of a series of publications called 'Malas'. Thus we find "Bakul Mala", "Swadhyaya Mala", "Balwangmaya Mala", "Kishor Sahitya" and others apart from individual titles published by other reputed publishers. Sonyabapu started a new series of children's books in 1938, named, "Shri Samarth Bal Sahitya", and till 1944 nearly 143 titles were published in this series by writers who were popular at that time. It appears that some of the first few titles were already published by others (and their publishers might have declined to reprint them). Thus Sonyabapu got a few available good titles to start with.

Another situation led to Dhawale's decision to purchase 'Karnatak'. Dhawale's major support in getting their publications printed was Mumbai Vaibhav Press, where the manager of the press, Bhasker Sidhaye, was extremely cooperative and accommodative. He expired in December 1940. His demise must have also influenced the decision of the Dhawales to look out for their own printing unit for the growing list of publications. Besides other publications they had already released nearly 158 children's books. Their books, though of 50 to 70 pages, had inputs in the form of illustrations, coloured covers, effective marketing etc. It was quite a taxing and time-consuming job. The Dhawales could not expect the same service from the new management of the Mumbai Vaibhav Press which had given them trusted support so far.

Sonyabapu, now about 30 years of age, thought of buying a printing unit. Another well-known printing unit, Tutorial Press, was also for sale but the negotiations with them were unsuccessful. Somewhat desperate to buy and also considering the size and the potential of the

Karnatak Press, Sonyabapu lapped up the opportunity when Mangesh, equally desperate to sell, offered it for sale.

Sonyabapu had another special attraction for Karnatak. It had a type foundry which cast types in the major languages of the region. Besides, the Karnatak Types in Devnagari were a marginal improvement on the types from the Javji Dadaji foundry. There is no record of the person or a group who had conceived, designed and implemented the improvements. In types a small, at times apparently inconsequential change in curvature, drops, length etc. of a font distinguishes one variety of type from another. In Roman types we find typographers constantly striving to design a more elegant and aesthetic type. Devnagari at that time offered little scope for such change. However, the 'Akhand Pica' developed by Karnatak was undisputedly a gift from its type foundry to the printing world. Needless to state, all that does not mean much in the present world of computers which can offer you numerous varieties.

We have also to rely on the word of those who were close to Sonyabapu to know about his deep study of typography. He had carefully observed the developments in this subject. In fact at some stage he discussed with his technicians the possibility of developing new punches for Devnagari types and was to order the equipment necessary for the purpose.

Just thirty now he had almost a decade of experience in publishing and interacting with printers of the city. In 1945, Sonyabapu became the supremo of almost an empire. Keshav Bhikaji Dhawale firm was already of a sizeable arena, and the addition of the other equally prestigious list of publications in English, Marathi,

Kannada and Gujarati, a type foundry, and the unencumbered asset of Karnatak House offered a truly golden opportunity for the artist, dreamer and innovator in Sonyabapu. His ambition knew no limits and he for the next few years – almost a decade and a half – thought of soaring heights, almost as an eagle does in the limitless vast, expansive skies. He worked for 18 hours a day normally. Probably he had the nuances of printing and publishing disturbing him in his dreams too. For, during this period he achieved a lot experimenting in colour printing. He launched several schemes. This was the most thrilling and glorious period and yet it was also a boisterous and trying period for him and his family.

We will record some of his achievements. But when we do so, we should note another development that took place, which was perhaps the beginning of his loss of control over his overambition, desire to overdo and his inability to face personal and financial problems.

Let us deal with his personal problems first. In any Indian family we do find differences of opinions, clash of interests and consequently a conflict amongst the members of a family-owned business. At times these do raise their heads to an extent that splits become inevitable. In such situations often members who are not directly involved in the business arrangements take unusual interest in the business and become instrumental in wrecking the smooth continuance of the personal relationships. However, the Dhawales were a small joint family with Keshav Bhikaji and nephew Sonyabapu and the daughter of the elder brother Mahadev having financial interest in the firm. They were all living together at Samarth Sadan. Later Sonyabapu shifted to Karnatak House in Chira Bazaar. The reason that was presented to the public was that it would be more convenient to look after the business from the workplace. It was, however, not that simple. Keshav Bhikaji who had all along backed the 'adventures' of his talented nephew, was unable to stem the tide of dissension. Though the official and final inevitable separation came in 1964, the fire was raging even earlier and it obviously affected Sonyabapu's composure too.

Purchase of 'Karnatak' was possible because of the backing of the Bank of Maharashtra which sanctioned the loan required. However, more funds were needed as working capital. These may have been provided by relatives and well-wishers. Popular Book Depot gave an advance of Rs. 50,000, a substantial amount at that time, with an understanding that it would be adjusted against the printing bills of the 'Popular' publications printed at Karnatak. Some of the best selling textbooks *Calculus* by Pavate and Bhagwat, *Intermediate Physics* in two volumes by D. S. Jog, *Inorganic Chemistry* by Nadkarni and Kothare and many more books, which had so far dull covers and just average printing quality got a new garb and certainly improved in production values because of the personal supervision of Sonyabapu. Thus the connection between Popular Book Depot (Ganesh Bhatkal) and Karnatak's Sonyabapu, which started in 1945 with the financial help of Rs. 50,000 lasted even after the press equipment and the foundry was sold.

With the advent of Independence in 1947, another important development took place which affected the fortunes of Karnatak considerably. There was the inevitable migration of individuals from India to Pakistan and the other way too. Owners of Samsher Printing Press owned by a Muslim family had set up a printing plant at

Sion where there were already two buildings for the plant and machinery and a warehouse. Attached to it was a three-storeyed residential building. The family was opting to go to Pakistan. Sonyabapu thought that this was another opportunity that he could not miss. He hurriedly entered into a lease agreement with Samsher Printing Press for three years. 'Karnatak' and ' Dhawale', which had more or less integrated or shall we say organised their publication programme, shifted in unison lock, stock and barrel from Chira Bazar to Sion.

Just a few years after Karnatak was purchased Sonyabapu's ambitions soared again. The large space of Samsher Printing Press at Sion was too much of a temptation for him. He was always thinking big. He acquired an offset printing machine from Siddha Litho Press. He added some new machines.

What is it that prompted him or motivated him to undertake such brave ventures? Some of these surely proved to be misadventures. Perhaps it was the burning desire to be big and to achieve something great. Otherwise he had hardly organized himself either financially or thought of setting up an administrative machinery when he entered into the short-term lease agreement with Samsher Printing Press at Sion. There was a small chance that the owner of this press may opt to migrate to Pakistan permanently and if that happened the property would be available at a reasonable price after the lease agreement ended. But the calculations proved wrong. Because of the huge influx of refugees from Pakistan to Bombay, the property prices shot up. The owners of the property decided to come back and demanded a price that Sonyabapu could not afford. Sonyabapu had no alternative but to move the press again to Chira Bazar. The shift to

Sion and back to Girgaon meant a huge loss and thus began the slide in the fortunes of Karnatak which could not be stemmed.

In the first place a number of working days were lost and so was the business. Worse was the loss of inventory due to pilferage, perhaps inevitable in an operation of this magnitude. It is difficult to imagine the work involved in transporting a stock of over 1500 publications, besides paper and the machines. Resetting of machines also presented a heavy load on the already depleted finances. It was said in those days that the pilferages made in this transit gave opportunity to a few unscrupulous persons to set up small bookshops of their own with the books available to them at low cost as it was a stolen stock.

During the few years that the unit operated at Sion new schemes were launched, many more new books

The Sion Unit (Editorial input)

published. The two publications that deserve special mention were The *Indian War of Independence* by *Swatantrayaveer* V. D. Savarkar and the three-volume set of *The History of Marathas* by renowned historian G. S. Sardesai. The production of these two books was comparable to the best of production anywhere in the world and was appreciated as such by knowledgeable persons. In this connection it should be mentioned that during this period Sonyabapu had a host of experts with him and he developed a full-fledged turn-key production unit. Anyone who visited the Sion establishment was struck by the layout of the establishment at the site. There was a mezzanine floor from where the boss lorded over his empire with his colleagues, like Sri. Ba. Ranade, the poet; G. D. Khanolkar, about whom we have already written; W. L. Kulkarni, a literary critic and educationist;

The Sion Unit (Warehousing and Distribution)

Satyabodh Hudlikar, an educationist; H. D. Dargalkar, a technician, who had returned from Germany after studying printing and block making; and the versatile genius, D. G. Godse, an artist, but a person of many interests; and some others like editors and proof-readers. Type foundry, typesetting, printing, block making, art department, binding and finally, the warehouse and sales department were so well positioned that the workflow became smooth.

A few other projects were undertaken which proved short-lived. A successful children's magazine *Khelgadi* was purchased from its editor and owner, K. R. Palvankar. A house journal *Iye Marathichiya Nagari* was started. A Sunday weekly *Rawiwar* was also launched. All these had a very short life though each one of them was a fine specimen of ideal production in every respect. A monthly *Dhawale* also failed to catch public attention. It seems, publications of periodicals could not be Karnatak's forte.

From 1950 to 1954, after the sad Sion experiment Sonyabapu had to face a spate of misfortunes. He was almost bedridden for about 14 months by a severe attack of sciatica. The firm lost nearly Rs. 1.75 lakhs in a fraud for which their own trusted finance manager was probably responsible. But it was so cleverly managed by the individual that it was not possible to trace the culprit and prove his complicity in this deed. There were other court cases like the copyright of the "Virkar Dictionary" which ended in a compromise that allowed Karnatak to produce the dictionary without using the name of Virkar's Dictionary. All this took time and energy and the firm lost money. It also meant considerable loss of business too.

But the worst blow was the rejection of thirty-eight

text-books for the 5th, 6th and 7th standards in all subjects. There was a change of syllabus in the fifth standard school curriculum. New manuscripts were prepared as per the new syllabus. Later some of these did get the nod but by then some other publishers had made inroads in the market. If one examines the contents and the production of these textbooks, one would concede that they had the highest standards from the point of selection of material, its presentation, suitable illustrations etc. They could be models of what an ideal textbook in the respective subject should be. The subjects they covered were language, mathematics, social science and pure science. This was certainly too heavy a loss that broke the back of the business. It was not only the loss of amount that was spent on the production of the books but also the loss of business. To recover from this huge loss one had to attract new business for the printing unit or think of new ventures.

Sonyabapu had more ideas, another dream. It had to be made into a reality. He launched a plan to produce books in five languages – "Panch Bhashik Yojana" – in Marathi, Gujarati, Kannada, Hindi and English. Different logos were designed for each language – *Shreedhar Prakashan* for Marathi, *Somnath Sahitya* for Gujarati, *Karnatak Prakashan* for Kannada, *Mayur Kitaben* for Hindi and *Phoenix Publications* for English. Variation in colophones was another of his speciality. He designed different colophones to indicate the nature of the publications – religious, children's books, books for adults, books for women, textbooks and books on astrology. *Buddha Charitra* was the first in the Panch Bhashik Yojana. Like the previous dreams this too failed to get off the ground.

During this period of trial and travail there was one redeeming event for which Karnatak could deservedly be proud of. It received an award for excellence in printing in the very first year of its institution of these awards by the Central Government. The book, *A Journey Through Toyland* by Kamalabai Dongerkery and illustrated by an Austrian, Ms. A. B. Schwartz, was adjudged as the best in the category of 'Illustrated Books'. The book was published by Popular Book Depot, and G. R. Bhatkal as the publisher and B. G. Dhawale as the printer received the awards in New Delhi at the hands of the President of India, Dr. Sarvapalli Radhakrishnan. Sonyabapu and myself put in considerable hard work, discussing and planning the book to make it a model of excellence in design and production. It was essentially an outstanding specimen of Sonyabapu's production skill. It was a coffee-table book in crown quarto size and the text was printed in deep grey and the illustrations were printed in colour to match the terracotta toys. The layout of the pages presented a pleasing visual, most suitable for the illustrations and the text. I remember that some of the blocks for the illustrations were done in several sizes and different layouts were tried out to achieve the desired end-effect. The end papers and the jacket were also designed to give the book a splendid display value. Special binding cloth was ordered which too gave the book the richness in its production. Altogether it was a triumph for the publisher and the printer and it came as a welcome relief to Sonyabapu at a time when he was facing unimaginable difficulties.

Textbook sales had depleted and most of the projects started by him met with rough weather. This situation needed to be changed. The machines which could give really huge output had to be fully utilized. Something that could feed the machines regularly had to be thought of to keep the machines running. This was the origin which gave birth to "Nandi Books". The idea was to publish a book a week, on a particular day in the format of Pocket Books, initially to be produced in Marathi and English but later in other Indian languages of the region too. Priced at 1 Rupee each it was expected to tap a wide market. Dhawale and Popular, joined hands and a new series named Nandi was born and with combined expertise in marketing of two publishers, the project was expected to achieve mammoth results. The first few titles were launched with a lot of fanfare at a gala function presided over by P. K. Atre, then at the height of his popularity. It was blessed by Mangesh Kulkarni, the former proprietor of Karnatak. Titles for English books were specially written or edited for the series while those for Marathi books mostly came from the Dhawale's cellar– manuscripts acquired by them earlier but which had remained unpublished. The print run for the first edition was 5000 copies. Today we will not find this number an attractive proposition. But we should go back to the day when a publisher could think of only 1000-1200 copies. An ultimate target of 10000 to 20000 copies of each book and two books a week and later a possibility of five books a week was visualized to keep a machine busy at least for 4 to 5 shifts a week. But this project also failed utterly, though the response was not too bad as most of the titles became out of print within a short time. Totally just twelve titles in Marathi and six in English were published in this series.

A few interesting episodes in connection with the Nandi Books scheme need to be recorded. The meeting convened to decide the name for the series was attended by Sonyabapu, Khanolkar and myself. The help of D. G. Godse, S. R. Tikekar, Prabhakar Goray and some others was also sought. The criteria were simple. With a view to having books in the major languages of India, we had to choose a symbol that was visually acceptable in the different regions of the country. Several names were suggested and discussed! After a few hours of discussion we zeroed on the symbol of the flower 'parijat'. Goray, the artist who was present at the meeting also prepared a specimen of the cover design. But then it was rejected and we could not accept it as it was too weak in its impact. We needed some symbol that was more heavy, prominent and attractive, assertive from the point of readers' response. So Nandi, the revered and widely known icon of Lord Shiva's Bull, found favour. However, our problem was not solved. The logo was to be used even in a diminutive size without losing the elegance, solidity and visual impact. So a search for such a Nandi began. Several temples were visited to see Nandi installed there. All available photographs of Nandis were collected. Finally Nandi in a sitting pose was approved.

Every effort was made to plan the series. For the first title in English we thought of a rewritten version of Aesop's Fables by Mulk Raj Anand, who along with Pupul Jaykar, was then editing a children's magazine *Clay Cart.* He was approached. He was at that time spending more time at his spacious farmhouse at Khandala. We met him there. A thorough professional writer, he gave the manuscript within a fortnight as promised. Apart from a well publicised publication ceremony, massive publicity material was produced and distributed with special attention given to the booksellers in small towns and smaller places.

Sonyabapu from 1949 onwards was, as we have observed, hardly consistent in pursuing the various innovative schemes launched by him. Always temperamental in nature, ill-heath had sapped his physical energy and a spate of recurrent misfortunes had affected his composure. The only factor that kept him moving was his undiminished enthusiasm, genuine desire to achieve some success in printing and publishing and his aptitude for appreciation of any aesthetic media. Few people know of his collection of art works. He continued to keep himself up-to-date by reading latest writings on the subjects in which he was interested.

Nandi Books probably could have met with better fate

Sonyabapu had a flair for using different logos for different genres of publications. These are some of a total of 23 that were identified.

'Nandi' Books release at Mafatlal Swimming Pool, Chowpatty, Mumbai. (From Left) : G. R. Bhatkal, Mangesh Kulkarni, P. K. Atre, G. D. Khanolkar, S. R. Tikekar and W. L. Kulkarni

than what they actually did if two persons who were connected with this series were able to contribute their inputs. One of them was Sonyabapu's elder son, Sriniketan, known by his pet name of Bandu. He had started taking interest in the firm's business recently and had picked up its intricacies reasonably soon. He was young, just out of his teens. But there was a setback to his involvement on account of a small incident. An insignificant mistake on his part brought for him a catastrophe when his father discovered the error. For Sonyabapu no error could be trivial. Losing his temper he gave a severe dressing down to Sriniketan in the office in the presence of a few colleagues. It was too shocking for the young man. He left his home and town without informing anyone. Perhaps he thought that when he went places he could do some introspection. The next few days were traumatic for the family. Search in different directions to find him as per the hunches of astrologers proved futile. Sriniketan returned after a few days when whatever cash he had taken with him was finished. But father-son relations had soured. He repeated the experiment. But this time he left a note while departing. He was, of course, in search of advice and guidance, which he received from a senior relative and friend of the family. This friend advised him properly and suggested that he should go back to his family and profession wherein lay his future. I remember the day when myself and my wife were summoned at midnight to celebrate the news, received by phone, that Sriniketan would be coming back. We were facing anxious, awestruck parents, who offered *pedhas* to us with the joyous news. After all, however harsh the father, he did have immense love for his children and faith in their capacity.

The other person who could have bolstered up Nandi Books was myself. But I was preoccupied with pressing engagements through the best part of 1959 and 1960, particularly in the Harvard International Seminar in Boston, and the later seminar in Japan where they had selected candidates from participants of previous seminars. There were several international book fairs and our own growing business to attend to. These were important for me for my personal and professional growth. Yet in the later part of 1960, again unexpectedly I had to make myself available for the rehabilitation of Karnatak. This was for me an exciting experience, one that enriched my own perceptions of business management and organizational skills.

9

Bhatkal and Chaudhari

A disaster for Karnatak Printing Press was averted in 1960 by two well-wishers of Karnatak, Bhatkal and Chaudhari.

Sonyabapu needed someone to interact with for his innovative ideas. Besides he enjoyed staying with friends around him. Khanolkar was already an important person in his life. Another person by his side was N. L. Chaudhari (Nana), who had by now retired from his construction business. He was an intimate member of the Dhawale household as he had constructed Samarth Sadan for them. He knew the family from the mid-30s. I was comparatively a new member of this small group of three. But from 1954 I too became so close to the two others that hardly a day passed when we did not meet. We were not so much used to using the telephone in those days and we could find some time for our own leisure and pleasure to meet in person. We were all gourmets. At Karnatak House we used to have the specially prepared tea, personally by Sonyabapu, and often homemade laddoos or rich sweets received through angadias – *Halvasan* from Khambayat or *Sutarfeni* from Surat. There were two eating joints frequented by us, Kwality at Worli and Tea Centre at Churchgate. At Tea Centre our menu was more or less fixed and the waiters also knew our choice. As soon as we occupied a table the favourite dishes were served. The waiters had only to ask us whether that particular day we preferred Darjeeling or Nilgiri tea.

Sonyabapu's major obsession was keeping himself up-to-date with developments all over the world about the subjects in which he was interested. He subscribed to most of the trade journals. These journals and books on printing and publishing were not just adornments of his library. He regularly referred to them and also constantly studied them. He regularly interacted with professional experts and senior colleagues in the profession.

He played a major role in two important events, both again short-lived. The first was the establishment of a distribution and promotion centre for books in Bombay and Pune in the mid-fifties with the cooperation of Continental Prakashan and Deshmukh & Company. In the other he became the Founder President of Marathi Granth Prakashan Sabha (1962), a publishers' association.

A memorial volume *Sonyache Divas* published soon after his death by his son has a reasonably unbiased assessment of Sonyabapu's strengths and more obvious failures in his life. Most of the writers have opined that Sonyabapu lacked in business acumen. It is not easy to agree fully on this judgement. It is true that post-1945 it was a downward slide for Karnatak which could not be stemmed. But there are two indications that tend to disprove the reading about his lack of abilities in management. He took complete charge of the business in 1938. Firstly when Karnatak was taken over by Keshav Bhikaji Dhawale in 1945, they had already developed sufficient assets that were considered adequate by the Bank to advance substantial funds. In fact two series – Samarth Sadan Prakashan (over 25 titles) and Samarth

Samarth Sadan, Girgaon

Sadan Bal Sahitya (nearly 125 titles) – were published and marketed successfully from 1938 to 1944. Besides they had rights for a number of reprints. Secondly, some of the records that were available and perused by us show that as a publisher his set-up could be described as ideal. Most of the manuscripts were sent for assessment to 'editors' or 'reviewers' – all experts in the subject. Costing was done as soon as any manuscript was accepted for publication. Royalty agreements were made as per the practice prevailing at that time – namely payment per page of the manuscript (unlike later system of royalty payment on a percentage basis of published price of the book). Constant review was undertaken periodically of the progress of the business. But the situation changed dramatically after 1945.

All this shows that Sonyabapu did have business acumen. He could manage the affairs of the business successfully and to face calamities when they arose. However, it is a fact that after 1950 he lost his grip over the situation. We would like to analyse the reasons for the same.

Firstly, it was clear that the downward slide had started way back in the mid-fifties when he had to face the triple loss of the Sion experiment, 1955 textbooks debacle and some important but futile court cases. He could not concentrate on work though there was enough business to attend to.

Right through this period the major problem that hastened the crisis was poor financial management. Cash flow, though substantial, was not adequate to meet the growing expenses. It was clearly a case of 'over trading' as it was known at that time. In any business the basic principle is to keep the expenses within the income level.

There may be temporary adjustments. However in Sonyabapu's case the temporary adjustments became semi-permanent obstacles and later permanent liabilities. These could not be liquidated except by disposing of assets. It is necessary to go into some details about the situation.

Sonyabapu had multiple sources for raising funds – bank loans, borrowing from friends and relatives, credit facilities from suppliers, and getting finance from the *hundi* market. Normally very few businessmen take advantage of credit from the *hundi* market unless they are perfect in budgeting and planning and have a good advisor for cash management. The pressure under which Sonyabapu worked from 1945 to 1962 prevented him from using his erstwhile skills. Added to that he felt the absence of moral support he always enjoyed from his uncle Keshav Bhikaji who expired on 1 December 1957.

Uncle Keshav never ever interfered in the business decisions of his nephew. On the contrary his response as reported was always "I am with you". One fails to understand the logic behind this *laissez-faire* policy. If he had cautioned and reined in Sonyabapu's over-enthusiasm perhaps we would have seen a more favourable course of events. But that was not to be. Sonyabapu always had his way even from his childhood days. However, he had high respect for his uncle and a little guidance from him occasionally would have changed matters.

With the demise of the patriarch there were two forces that must have made the situation worse. First the pressure from the household. This must have been so unbearable that around this time (1959-60) Sonyabapu shifted his residence from Benham Hall Lane (Samarth

Sadan) to the top floor of the press building in Chira Bazar. The younger lot, two sons and two daughters joined him.

The other and more significant pressure was from the Bank of Maharashtra where the loan instalments to be paid by Karnatak became more and more irregular. Matters came to a head when a dutiful officer of the Bank summoned Sonyabapu to the bank for pressing him to regularise the loan instalments. Possibly he might have been a little harsh during the talk. Deeply hurt and true to his inherent trait of not accepting such treatment he told the officer that he will pay the due instalments forthwith and that the officer should realize that Sonyabapu was the owner of a prestigious enterprise while the officer was only a mere employee. With the help of his legal advisor K. M. Gokhale he approached a financier who gave him the amount instantly. We were told that he was given currency notes stacked just under the mattress of his bed where he was seated. The Bank officer was stunned when the amount was paid within a few hours of the unhappy incident. He also had to listen to the harsh words from his chief though the senior officer must have been, we can be sure, happy that the junior had carried out his duty in the best interest of the Bank He certainly deserved a pat on his back from his seniors for his successful encounter with a difficult client.

This finance came with a heavy burden of exorbitant interest. The only security was the reputation of the Dhawale family as certified by solicitor Gokhale. Seeing that the advance could not be repaid in the near future and to avoid the burden of the mounting interest, the family sold an open plot of land they had near Samarth Sadan and freed themselves of further trouble on this issue. Apparently the elder members of the family and their advisors must have found further ground to talk about the rash ventures of Sonyabapu and his business management about which they must have their reservations.

A similar situation had to be faced with regard to the funds borrowed from the *hundi* market. This is an interesting market. We had studied about it in our class on economics even when we were undergraduates. But we must admit that it is much more exciting and exacting than what we learnt from the textbooks. We will give the details of transactions involved later on. Suffice it to state that it is a useful arrangement only for temporary accommodation of financial crunches or when one has planned thoroughly both short and long-term aspects of income, expenditure and profit of a venture. We will see how and when we tackled the players in this market.

I was participating in the Harvard International Seminar in Tokyo in 1960 when I got a message from my friend and chartered accountant M. P. Chitale that I should return to Bombay early to solve a crisis at Karnatak. Since I had no inkling of the gravity of the situation (as at least when I left Bombay there was no sign of such a calamity) I rang up home to let me know whether I should curtail my further itinerary which included an extended tour of a few south-east Asian countries. The reply brought cheer for me as it said that though the situation was serious it could wait for 10 to 12 days and I could complete my tour. But for me there was both suspense and tension during this period as communication was then not as easy as it is now. Besides I was to visit six countries and would always be on the move. So I had to wait till I returned to Bombay to get all the details of the crisis.

Sonyabapu had continued the Karnatak tradition of borrowing from the *hundi* market – a practice that was being followed by Mangeshrao too before 1945. In fact I had a very flitting experience of signing some *hundis* for Mangeshrao when I was asked by my father to do so as a partner of Popular Book Depot. Perhaps he was introducing me to a possible source of finance if we were in dire need of it or he wanted to introduce me to the system of being helpful to a friend in need, in this case Mangeshrao of Karnatak.

All these transactions were being negotiated for Sonyabapu by an agent, Nandlal Chugamal. Sonyabapu did not have to stir out of his cabin. In fact, besides the signing of the *hundi* paper he did not have to do anything except to tell Nandlal if and when some additional funds were required. Sadly the question of reducing the liability did not arise for Karnatak during this period. This Dhawale-Nandlal arrangement ran smoothly over a decade.

In 1959-60, Nandlal entered into film production and his maiden production flopped. He himself was in trouble. He told Sonyabapu that he could not be of help any more. Further a *hundi* or two which were due to be renewed had to be paid in cash. The only alternative available being sale of a machine or two, which were mortgaged to the Bank of Maharashtra. This would have been both immoral and illegal.

Chitale who was a well-wisher of Dhawales and also an advisor to the Bank suggested that now the time had come to alert the Bank of Maharashtra too. The Bank thought of taking immediate action of foreclosing the mortgage. At this point Chitale thought, perhaps a change of management could save Karnatak and the Bank should hold on if someone could take up this task. M.P.Chitale was introduced to Popular Book Depot by Sonyabapu in 1956, when we had to face a difficult taxation problem. A reputed Chartered Accountant he became our financial advisor too. A voracious reader, he loved books. He was not much senior to me in age and he and I had common interests. We spent sometime together in the evenings discussing new books and also political, social and economic matters. He visited Popular Book Depot almost every evening while returning to his residence from his office. He had studied in depth Popular's business policies as well as its progress. He felt that I could handle the Karnatak problem competently. He thought of me for this onerous responsibility and had sent the message to me in Tokyo. The Bank was willing to wait for a short time.

Immediately on my return I started assessing the ground situation. The Bank loan was fully secure. The borrowings from the *hundi* market by then had gone up to nearly five lakhs. The dues to suppliers and authors' royalties, though considerable, were within a manageable limit. I felt confident of handling the situation. Decisions had to be taken fast and implemented with a firm hand. The only area to which I was a stranger was the *hundi* finance. I had of course read about this market in the textbooks. But the ground situation was different. I somehow had a hunch that the grand old man, Mangeshrao (from whom Dhawales had purchased the Karnatak unit), who had introduced the system to Karnatak and who was my mother's uncle could help. He told me to approach the shroffs – the lenders – directly and explain to them that since their advances were without any security they will not get back anything if the Bank took action. He further advised that they may be offered 50 per cent of their dues if they settled the *hundis* in full settlement.

The *hundi* market is a very interesting one. The shroffs are a united lot having a common intelligence system which assesses every borrower's worth in his business or rather in the market. But these financiers (shroffs) are very considerate and helpful. If for instance your need is of Rs. 10 lakhs and you are worth only 5 lakhs they will give you the additional 5 lakhs in the name of any of your relatives or friends whose worth is also assessed by them beforehand. Thus about half of the advance given to Sonyabapu was in the name of Nana Chaudhari, a good friend, a landlord owning property in Vasai, suburb of Mumbai, and with some furniture business that he got from his brother, A. L. Chaudhari & Co.

Thus, Nana and myself, as advised by Mangeshrao, went on the 'pilgrimage' visiting the dens of the shroffs, which were housed in a couple of old buildings near Mumbadevi Temple. Each floor had a few large rooms where a dozen or more shroffs sat in good old style with *takias* to relax and *gaddis* covered with surf-white bedsheets, each having by his side a desk where the documents were kept. Apparently they had different rules and norms for different types of advances they gave. We were told that this group had unlimited funds at their disposal. It was also said that in good old days their ancestors were able to finance the rulers in Delhi when they were in dire need. What is described here is from my personal experience.

As mentioned earlier *hundies* of about five lakhs of rupees had to be paid off as renewal was unthinkable and impossible too as the market already knew about

Karnatak's present status.

Nana Chaudhari and myself were advised by Mangeshrao that we could offer 50 per cent of the *hundi* amount to the shroffs which would perhaps satisfy them. He had remarked "Well! They have earned from Karnatak much more in the past years!" This approach did work. It meant hard work as the five lakhs debt was from scores of shroffs who were sitting in different rooms on different floors and in three different buildings. We could muster part of the funds from daily receipts from business. Yet we needed two lakhs which we were able to get from the Bank of Maharashtra. We persuaded them to trust us as they had accepted us as guarantors for Karnatak. We assured them that instalments to the Bank will be regularly paid. Chaudhari and Bhatkal will take over the management of the entire business.

The first important and tough decision was apparently not a pleasant one. Sonyabapu, a real and good friend of both of us, had to be told to vacate the chair he had occupied with aplomb in the office for several years. He had also to be firmly but politely told that from now on each and every decision would be taken by us (in actual practice it was by me as I had some experience of the printing house economics). Accustomed to having his own way all these years, he was not pleased. He was even hurt. Luckily he did not raise any doubts about our intentions. We assured him, however, that we would give a daily report of the transactions to him. Since someone was required to manage minute-to-minute workflow at the press and also to ensure Sonyabapu's confidence we requested Sriniketan, Sonyabapu's eldest son to help us in the management. He had from 1956 been helping his father. Level-headed but still a little immature he could be depended upon to deliver the goods.

The plan that I had chalked out for the rehabilitation of the business was meticulously outlined. Our first priority was to liquidate the advances with heavy interest from *hundiwallas*. Except for a solitary hard nut, we were able to settle the account of others at fifty percent of the advance, though a couple of them had to be paid a little more. The second priority was the instalments to the Bank. The suppliers were few and most of them agreed to our suggestion that on fixed days they would be paid some instalment depending on the funds available. Only one of them, who perhaps was hurt at some time by the management, filed a suit. We ignored him altogether as we were confident that we could pay him before the case came up for hearing or we could get a decision from the court to accept more or less our scheme of payment. We thought that the authors could wait for their royalty dues as for most of them writing was not their daily bread. Karnatak dues to Popular Book Depot who were advancing monies to them regularly also got a low priority for obvious reasons.

Sriniketan helped us for nearly two to three months. The arrangement was working out smoothly. But soon another hard decision had to be taken to even ask Sriniketan to quit. To be fair to him it must be said that he was also facing a dilemma when he paid some amount as part royalty to an author, a family friend of his, when he pressed him hard to do so considering his urgent need. But our schedule was upset thereby and the plan could go awry.

Krishna Kurwar, then working in our publishing unit and a senior member of our staff, replaced Sriniketan. Kurwar felt indebted to Karnatak for the rich experience he got during this period as also during a short time he worked with Sonyabapu after we handed over the management back to him.

For me it was an exciting and enriching experience though it was very hard work. It was a period when I was active in our own business expansion, involved in strengthening the Federation of Publishers and Booksellers Association in India, and was undertaking many tours within and outside the country; besides, I was connected with several other activities. It, however, gave me immense satisfaction as I was participating in an experiment of rehabilitating a sick unit, helping a good friend to regain confidence to rebuild his ambitious empire and assessing my own strength to handle challenging situations.

Thanks to co-operation received from everyone concerned and our meticulous planning we were able to achieve our goal within less than one and half years. We had added two lakhs to our liabilities by borrowing from the Bank but in about fifteen months we were able to meet our commitments as per promises made by us. Bank instalments were regularly paid, creditors got their dues as per schedules and total liabilities were reduced by at least Rs. 4 lakhs. The documents pertaining to the transactions were preserved by us till recently. We destroyed them as old files were becoming unmanageable. An analysis of those papers would have provided a worthwhile case study of how a sick unit could be revitalized within a short time with perfect planning and firm determination.

For me and Nana it was a satisfying experience and more importantly we derived the pleasure of helping a dear friend when he needed our assistance and confidence most. When Nana and myself, after a year of our management of the affairs of Karnatak, decided to request Sonyabapu to take over, we had some reservations and trepidations. The reservation was with regard to obtaining permission from the Bank which had a bitter experience of this account in the past. Ultimately we were able to persuade them to agree to the change. We had to use the good offices of Chitale again for this purpose. We assured the Bank that the matters were really under control and we did not expect that the future would present any problems. The worry was on account of the apprehensions that Sonyabapu, after his return to his desk, may again be indiscreet and repeat his mistakes, his misadventures and miscalculations, which certainly was a possibility. But the events in the next 5 to 6 years proved that our fears were unwarranted.

A year's absence from active involvement in the Press must have given Sonyabapu enough time for introspection. His twenty odd years as head of the Karnatak-Dhawale empire was indeed 'a crowded hour of glorious life'. He had his dream projects; many of them had brought glory to himself and the institution. Some failed miserably. He did not wish to get himself involved any more in such mishaps. Enough is enough he must have thought. He was nearing fifty years of his life and perhaps had an inkling of the future he had to face. He had few responsibilities to attend to. Surely he had some personal domestic duties to perform. He had eight children, four sons and four daughters. The eldest daughter was already married. During the four years, 1962-65, Sonyabapu must have felt relieved when he arranged for the wedding of his three daughters and also performed the thread ceremonies of the boys. By the end of this period he was already a proud grandfather of five kids.

It was time to attend to the smooth working of the business. He decided to concentrate on the printing business more rather than on publication of books of his own. He printed a Marathi translation of Old and New Testament on India paper, an excellent and difficult piece of printing. So far printing on this super-thin paper was mostly done abroad. The printing had to ensure that there is no see-through. It had also to stand comparison with the Bibles printed abroad. Karnatak came out with flying colours in this job. He also attended to work given to him by Popular Prakashan, Taraporewala and Bharatiya Vidya Bhavan. A few other smaller jobs also were acclaimed as models of excellent printing.

Another decision he took was a painful one but nevertheless inevitable. Most of the members of the Dhawale family were unhappy about the development of events after Karnatak was bought over by Dhawales. They felt that the decision to purchase Karnatak was entirely that of Sonyabapu. Again Keshav Bhikaji Dhawale publications, which had a smooth run of the business for 45 years were in trouble only after the Karnatak takeover. The only solid support that Sonyabapu had in the family, that of Keshav, was no more. Thus in 1964 Sonyabapu separated from the combine. He became the sole proprietor of Karnatak and relinquished his partnership in the Keshav Bhikaji Dhawale firm, where both his elder sons Sriniketan and Dhananjay had now joined. It was not an easy decision to make. After all for over twenty-five years he had participated in the growth of the family concern. He had taken it out of the narrow field of publications of books on religion and philosophy and widened it to include literature of all genre. Though a few books for children like Books of Alphabets, Books of Numbers were published earlier, it was Sonyabapu who had ventured to publish scores of well-edited, beautifully-designed, illustrated children's books. Publication of books for adult literates was also his idea. All this and the Karnatak unit had brought glory to the firm Keshav Bhikaji Dhawale. It is not possible for us to know whether he was forced to take this decision or after the recent events he thought of this inevitable solution which would lead to a smooth management of the family concern by his successors without any hindrances and without his intervention. Whatever that may have prompted him to take this step it was a rational decision, though, we can be sure, he must have been unhappy to sever his connection with the firm.

Physically because of severe diabetes his health was shattered. The above-described events shattered his confidence too. Again he must have thought of his own future and that of his two younger sons, who were in their teens. Once he made up his mind he worked for it relentlessly and with vigour. For once he seems to have made a plan for his retirement. First priority was to get rid of his liabilities because he would not like to end his life as a debtor. This could be done only by selling off his assets. Taking permission from the Bank he sold his type foundry and then the machines one by one. The process was completed by 1966 and in 1968 he sold the premises too and shifted his residence with his wife and two sons to Malad, a suburb of Mumbai. The Karnatak goodwill still remained with him.

10

Epilogue

We are now at the end of one chapter and at a beginning of a new one.

Sonyabapu breathed his last on 26 May, 1973. He had, as noted earlier, started winding up his shop and had completed it by 1968. As it happens in many cases the very thought of retirement makes one dull, inactive and idle-minded. But for Sonyabapu, who was in the habit of working for long hours, often for eighteen hours, it was unthinkable. During the period when he had slowed down on home production, he had still published nearly twenty publications. One of these was a 21-part 'Complete Works of Swami Vivekanand' in Marathi. It was a centenary year offer. These were produced in paper-back format. This series could be a revenue yielding item in a publisher's list. It was proved by the fact that it has had a few reprints so far. He also produced three books in pocket book format with a new Logo 'Ninad Pustaken'

Professionally he participated in another activity, namely, the formation of a professional body 'Marathi Granth Prakashan Sabha'. He contributed a great deal in drafting its constitution and he must have been delighted to be its founder President.

Even after he had no printing equipment of his own during 1966-68 he brought out nearly 40 publications.

One of them needs a special mention. It was a collection of poems by a poet till then not much noticed by readers. Sonyabapu had read a poem in a little-known magazine and he was so much impressed by it that he contacted the poet for publishing the collection of his poems. He was impressed not only by the quality of the verses but the thought content in them. He felt that the poem *Dukha mazhe rangale* he had read (It was the title of the book too.) reflected his own thoughts, his own struggles and emotions. The title of the poem which can loosely be translated as "There is pleasure in my pain" appealed to him and also to the readers who normally go through similar experience in their own lives.

Though it is difficult to catch the spirit of the poem I shall attempt a free rendering of the same in English.

Dreaming of soaring starry skies
Shattered lay my mature moments
Dark night to echo my moans
Surely there is pleasure in my pain

Unable to share my grief
Suffering many taunts and threats
Prancing failures as my pals
Do I regret my loneliness?

Sooted floundering flame as companion
Am lustreless, sapless
Severing my links with fate
Embraced resultant, residual grief

Unable to cross the surging storm
Or reach the safety of the bank
Wingless, sans radar
My dreams broke in billion pieces.

Sonyabapu Dhawale receiving National award for 'Excellence in printing' from Dr. Sarvapalli Radhakrishnan

Sriniketan Dhawale who is keeping the flag aloft

This book was also hailed as a model of superb production – colour scheme, layout, typography and format. It was possible for Sonyabapu to achieve this excellence as Mohan Mudranalaya managed by Krishna Kurwar was at his disposal and he could monitor every stage of the production. Kurwar was his protege and treated Sonyabapu as his guru.

After two or three years at Malad he was again restless. Learning that Rashtra Vaibhav Press was winding up and a few machines were available his desire to own a printing plant of his own resurged and for a very short time he set it up in Marol Industrial Estate. Luckily it was a short lease arrangement and he gave up the attempt within a year. Here he was able to print and publish the monumental work, the 151st book Bharat Gaurav Granthmala's *Sahitya Simha* a biography of Shripad Krishna Kolhatkar, the well-known dramatist, by G. D. Khanolkar.

By this time, harassed by various ailments, particularly most acutely by serious diabetes, his health was completely shattered. So too his enthusiasm. He probably also had a premonition about his ultimate destiny. He opted to go to Pune to stay with his eldest son Sriniketan, who was managing Samarth Granth Bhavan, originally started as a part of the Keshav Bhikaji Dhawale firm but which had now separated from the parent company and had become an independent unit.

Here too, he could not stall the deterioration in his health and succumbed to his illness within a few months of stay there. Thus ended the life of an ambitious, daring, enthusiastic, hard-working, art-loving genius who left behind a legacy any printer or publisher could learn from.

The Karnatak saga does not end here. There was a gap of some time when there could not be any publication of books with this imprint. Sonyabapu had become the sole owner of the Karnatak firm on 23 February, 1964, when the partnership with other family members was dissolved. After his demise in 1973, his wife Sarala became the owner by common consent of the legal heirs. She had for some time, lost all interest in worldly life, and spent some time in a religious organization. Later for a few years, she did come back to the family and was taking some interest in trying to arrange the vast collection of old records and collection of file copies of the Karnatak and Dhawale publications. This work, however, was not completed.

After her demise, again by common consent, the ownership seems to have devolved on Sriniketan, the eldest son of the family. He was operating from Pune at Samarth Granth Bhavan. This decision, that he could now use the Karnatak logo and be its owner, must have been taken after 2000, the centenary year of Keshav Bhikaji Dhawale. Since 2000, he has published 26 new titles that include five English books and reprinted 19 from the old list. This list presents a variety of subjects – novelettes, biographical stories, scientific books and plays. The emphasis still appears to favour books for children and young adults.

The models left for posterity by Sonyabapu will inspire anyone who is keen on quality productions. One of the recent publications issued by Sriniketan, *The Antarctic Expedition* in Marathi is a good example that can be cited in support of this statement.

And thus, we can be sure, the Karnatak flag will still fly high though ultimately it may suffer the fate of all such family-owned businesses which wither away sooner or later.

Appendix I

Publishers' Logos

Publishers' logos and a meaningful motto inscribed with it display the character of the publishing programme and policy. The logos designed and used by various Indian publishers during the last couple of centuries will make a fascinating study.

We propose to note the significance of the extremely imaginative and artistic logo of Karnatak; not only because it was perhaps one of the pioneering uses of the same to denote the nature of the list but because of the deep thought and significance of its design.

We find an earlier design in a series of books called *Vivekananda Yanche Samagra Khand* in several volumes that has a sketch of sunrise and the motto :

Let the lamp of knowledge be always bright. These were published during the second decade of the twentieth

century – the earliest volume could be traced to 1925.

Almost in the same year, 1925, we have another logo used in the multi-volume series of publications *Bharat*

नहि ज्ञानेन सदृशं पवित्रोमिह विद्यते।

Gaurav Granthmala which has the motto :

'There is nothing like knowledge in the world,' a line from Shloka 38, Chapter IV of Shrimad Bhagwad Gita alongwith a sketch of a profile of Srikrishna.

And finally, we find a magnificent logo with a sketch which evokes multi-faceted ideas in the minds of the readers. We were curious to probe into the possible meaning that the publisher and his designer of this logo wanted to convey. The logos I refer to were the products of the time when Mangeshrao Kulkarni was at the peak of his career. He did have with him a galaxy of erudite scholars and authors who could advise him on the motto. The names that come to our mind are Dada Gogate, the translator of Vivekananda and G. D. Khanolkar.

But the artist who sketched the design reproduced by us and which Karnatak used at least since 1925 to date needed to be studied. We requested our artist-scholar friend Vasant Sarawate to give an explanatory opinion.

He has given us a thought-provoking analysis of the mottos.

He writes:

"I will not be able to tell who might have conceived the idea of this logo, nor will I be able to name the artist who might have sketched it. But I would like to make an attempt to grasp the meaning of the logo as well as what it conveys to the viewers and the readers. With some sincere effort in this direction I think I have been able to come to a reasonable explanation. The logo says: 'नहि ज्ञानेन सदृशं पवित्रोमिह विद्यते।'

"This is from Ch. IV - Sholka 38 of the Bhagwad Gita. The next part of the sholka reads: 'तत् स्वयं योगसंसिद्धः कालेनात्मनी विन्दती!'

"This in translation means, 'There is nothing which can be more perfect and pure than knowledge.' Intellectuals and thinkers recognise that this knowledge can be obtained from self-analysis. Accordingly, they work towards this goal of knowledge. Here knowledge does not imply all that which is commonly known in this physical world. It, in fact, is 'self-realisation'. This entire Chapter IV is devoted to explaining the importance of self-realisation. And Chapter V is devoted to describing how this self-realisation can be achieved by certain as well as some positive action. Having stressed the importance of these two methods, Chaper VI makes available to the sadhaka the means available to attain self-realisation. *Kundalini Shakti* is a unique way of this yogic exercise. And it is true that self-realisation is possible. The ways in which it can be undertaken are explained in detail in this chapter.

"*Kundalini Shakti* is approximately near the spinal cord adjacent to the navel. The spinal cord, which is serpentine in structure, has to be activated from the bottom of the spinal cord through six stages which have to be passed before it reaches the brain. These stages are supposed to be in the form of a lotus.

And they are named as

1. Muladhar Chakra : 4 petals
2. Swadhishthan Chakra : 6 petals
3. Manipur Chakra : 10 petals
4. Anahat Chakra : 12 petals
5. Vishuddha Chakra : 16 petals
6. Adnya/Agnya Chakra : 2 petals

Logo 1925

Logo 1999 onwards

"These stages when activated generate the following reaction in the sadhaka.

The reactions are on :

1. The glands generating male & female hormones
2. Knowledge about earlier births
3. Speech
4. Mind and brain. It is possible that because of this you can control your mind and influence others.

5. Sensitivity to sound.
6. You can see beyond the normal vision. Also get consciousness of distant sounds. You can relate things from the past to possible happenings in the future.

"As we have a closer look at the logo, we find the sketch of the lotus in the center as well as on its two sides. There are two such lotuses in symmetry. These lotuses on the sides have 12 petals which are related to *Anahat Chakra*, while the one in the center has 16 petals which can be related to *Vishuddha Chakra*.

"I feel that the logo has this connection to the process of activating *kundalini* and consequently attaining self-realisation."

Appendix II

The Karnatak Press Families

Nadkarnis

Gotra : Kaundinya, Family God : Mangesh, Palavi God : Mahalakshmi.

The Nadkarni family is the oldest among the Saraswats that came to reside in North Kanara to the south of the Gangavali River. This family formed a branch of that Nadkarni family of Ankola. In the family partition between the two branches, the lands in the Andle and Joog villages came to the share of this family and as Bankikodla was nearer to these villages for management, the family settled at the place. In the partition between the Senior and Junior branches of Nadkarnis of Bankikodla the Andle Village went to the share of the former and the Joog to that of the latter.

The Gangavali River to the south of Ankola formed the boundary between the old kingdoms of Keladi and Sonde. Bankikodla then was under a Keladi Officer having his headquarters at Mirjan, and the whole territory under the jurisdiction of that officer upto the Gangavali River was known as Mirjan Shime. (The Chandavar Shime came to the South of the Mirjan River). The Nadkarnikars of Bankikodla, especially of the junior branch, were therefore known as Mirjan Shime

Nadkarnikars. The name was appropriated later on by the Junior branch of the family.

Nadkarni and Kulkarni were the names of certain revenue officers and were acquired by the remote ancestors of the present families of the Saraswats while in Goa about the eleventh century A.D.

The Nadkarni family seems to have settled in Bankikodla about the beginning of the fourteenth century and the Kulkarni family which followed it in the fifteenth century settled in Hanehalli about a mile from Bankikodla. The Balwalli family came there about the sixteenth century. Other families which settled there came from the south from among the Saraswats who had settled in the Kanaras.

The Nadkarni family branched off several times. The Gokarnkars who formed a branch of the Nadkarnis were the first to leave the family house and on account of a certain insult received from the elder stepbrother they renounced the surname and even their claim to the family estate. Next, there was a division between the Senior and Junior branches of the family, and then between the two branches of the junior family, one of the latter being designated Keremane or Chowkimane Nadkarni. Thus there are three main branches in the family excluding the Gokarnkars, and they are designated as Senior, Junior and Keremane. In subsequent years there were numerous subdivisions among each of these main branches, e.g. eight in the Senior branch, some sixteen in the Junior and seven in the Keremane branch. The process went on in later years and now there are more than two hundred families among the Nadkarnis. It forms the biggest family in the whole community even excluding the Gokarn branch. All the three branch families have retained their old surname in spite of the fact that there are several secondary surnames by which the sub-branches are distinguished mostly based on the villages where they own property. Only one small branch has in recent years begun to call itself Masur where it owns its share of the family property.

After the branching out into the three main divisions mentioned above, the Junior branch acquired much property and there were several partitions in this branch. With the help of the partition deeds and other evidence it has been possible to prepare a genealogy of this branch up to the 13th or 14th degree. Similarly a connected genealogy has been prepared of the Keremane branch. Of the Senior branch, though the genealogies of its eight sub-branches are available, it has not been possible to trace their ancestry to the Junior branch. Under the circumtances it has become impossible to connect the three main branches namely, the Senior, the Junior and the Keremane, and these three with Gokarnkars.

Each main branch of the family has got its own family God which holds certain property set apart during the family partitions. Temples are built by the main branches and a regular priest is appointed to perform the daily worship. The following are the temples built by the Nadkarnikars:

1. Chidanandeshwar Temple at Gokarn : Senior Nadkami. The priest is a Havik Brahman.

2. Varadrajeshwar Temple at Gokarn : Junior Nadkarni. The Priest is Ganesh Mangesh Bhat.

3. Vishweshwar Temple at Gokarn : Junior Nadkarni. The priest is Kaikini Vithal Bhat.

Bankanatheshwar Temple at Bankikodla belongs to all the local Saraswats. It was in a dilapidated condition when the Nadkarnikars came to Bankikodla but they rebuilt and endowed it.

(a) The Senior Nadkarnis have placed their family gods in a small temple built in the compound of Mr. Devappa Mangesh Nadkarni (Puttayya Shenai) worshipped by a priest of Bankikodla Bhat family.

(b) The family god of the Junior Nadkarnis is in the house of Mr. Ganesh Anant (Appu) Nadkarni at Bankikodla and worshipped by a priest of Bankikodla Bhat family.

(c) The family god of the Keremane Nadkarnis is in the house of Mr. Shankar Anandrao Nadkarni and worshipped by the Kagal Bhats.

The Junior branch of the family acquired a large expanse of landed property especially through the exertions of a member named Venkateshayya. He used to acquire extensive waste lands in different villages from the Government and bring them under cultivation and appoint different members of his family to live on or near those estates to look after them. Many of them were *gaznis* i.e. Salt lands drained of salt water and then used for producing inferior rice. This branch of the family at one time was looked upon as the richest in the community owning lands in the Talukas of Kumta, Honavar and Bhatkal. The family made large grants to the Mahableshwar Temple at Gokarn and to the family god at Mangeshi in Goa. In later years a trust was created for the administration of these charity funds.

Salt Works : Salt works existed in several places in North Kanara, such as : Sanikatta, Manki, Bailur, Shirali etc. It is during the time of the British Government that they have been concentrated at Sanikatta and those in other places are closed. The Sanikatta works consist of pans in four villages of Bidrageri, Nagarbail, Gonehalli and Kadme. The Nagarbail pans went to the share of the Senior Nadkarnis, Gonenalli pans to the Junior branch and later on most of them went to the share of the Keremane branch. The pans in Bidrageri and Kadme are very few and are held by all and sundry. A cooperative society of the owners of the pans was formed about twenty-five years ago for the better management of the works.

The Nadkarnis have a tradition to the effect that a couple known as Anant and Shanta were their progenitors, that Shanta had become a Sati on the funeral pyre of her husband Anant, that certain parts of her sari *(kapad)* tucked to the stomach *(niri)* had remained unburnt and also one lemon and a small stick known as *betkadi* taken by her while mounting the pyre had also remained entirely unburnt, and that these unburnt articles viz, part of sari *(kapad),* the lemon and the *betkadi* were preserved by the family as relics and were worshipped along with the household god. When the Nadkarnis were divided into four main branches, viz. Senior and the Junior branches and the Gokarnkars and the Junior again gave rise to a branch known as Keremane, it is said that these articles were preserved by all these four branches as heirlooms. Though these articles were said to have been preserved intact until recently there are very few even among the older generation who have actually seen them. The Kulkarni family of Bankikodla also alleges to have a similar tradition, but it is difficult to imagine that the families of Kulkarni and Nadkarni which belong to quite distinct stocks can have the same common ancestors. There is a tradition that the Nadkarnis of Bankikodla and Ankola observed *sutak* a long time ago but no traditon exists that Nadkarnis and Kulkarnis of Bankikodla had at any time observed *sutak*. It seems that these traditions and certain ceremonies performed by the members of these families such as *vaddapa* to propitiate their ancestors were aftergrowths. It is awkward to probe into the old beliefs of any family and it is only with apology that the above remarks are offered.

The Nadkarnis, Gokarns and Kulkarnis perform an important ceremony called *vaddapa* which literally means serving food in the name of ancestors. Many other families also perform *vaddapa* but in their case it lasts only a few minutes and is performed every year. But in the case of Nadkarnis it usually lasts for six days, and is invariably accompanied by *devakarya*. The *devakarya* commences on Monday in honour of God Mangesh, the following Tuesday is celebrated in honour of Anant-Shanta when an old pair (husband and wife) is to be worshipped. On Wednesday the ceremony is performed in the name of the lady of the family who died before her husband, on Thursday the Guru is honoured, on Friday the Devi is honoured and on Saturday Venkataraman of Tirupati is to be honoured. The six-day ceremony is observed only in one family. Others have curtailed the number of days.

The *vaddapa* and *devakarya* are to be performed not annually but before the *munja* or marriage of any member in the family and the performance is to take place in the family house and in the presence of the family god. As the members of the family are now spread over a wide area, the ceremony has often to be postponed and two or more such *vaddapas* have had to be combined into one.

How the custom of one family sometimes spreads among others is evidenced by the fact that the

Dhareshwar family of Kaundinya Gotra (not the branch of Ubhaya family called by that name) have been observing the same kind of *vaddapa* as that observed by Nadkarnikars but it lasts in their case for two days only, viz. *devakarya* on Monday and *vaddapa* on Tuesday. They allege to be a branch of the Nadkarni family. After carefully going through the matter it is found that the same kind of *vaddapa* is observed not only by the above mentioned family of Dhareshwar but also by the families of Kesarkodi and Hosangadi and that the first two families are branches of Hosangadi and not of Nadkarni family. There is moreover no tradition of Anant-Shanta in the case of these families.

Kulkarnis

Gotra : Kaundinya. Family God : Mangesh. Palavi God : Mahalakshmi.

The Kulkarni family came to Bankikodla via Ankola about a century after the Nadkamis went there i.e. in the fifteenth Century A.D., but settled in the neighbouring village of Hanehalli.

This family also maintains the tradition, as in the case of Nadkarnis, that Anant and Shanta were their progenitors and that Shanta became Sati on the funeral pyre of her husband Anant. This is the basis of the elaborate *vaddapa* ceremony observed in the family as is done by the Nadkarnis. But in recent years, one branch of the Kulkarnis has curtailed the number of days of the ceremony to two.

The Kulkarni family has built no temple. The household God of one branch is in the residence of the Angadi branch and of the other branches is in charge of the sons of Fouzdar Venkateshayya.

The Nadkarnis and Kulkarnis of Bankikodla do not come from the same family for reasons stated in the note on the Nadkarni family.

The distant *dayadis* of the Kulkarni family are to be found among the Kulkarnis of Avarsa in the Ankola Taluka.

Dr. Vishveshwarrao Kulkarni was a homoeopath of repute and he built a large business in that line in Bombay under the name of Roy & Co.. He also founded The Bombay Homoeopathic Medical Association and started a Homoeopathic College. All his concerns are being conducted by his sons. He wrote several books in English as well as in Marathi on Homoeopathy and some philosophical books in Sanskrit.

The name Kulkarni is associated with another flourishing business of Bombay, *viz.,* The Karnatak Printing Press which, being acquired by the late Mr. Ganpatrao Kulkarni, is now ably conducted by his brother, Mangeshrao.

Dhawales

Dhawales hail from Velwand, a place in the Ratnagiri District of Maharashtra. Their source of income was agriculture and money-lending. They enjoyed a fairly comfortable living. But Bhikajipant suffered some heavy losses and since then they had to face financial difficulties. The family shifted to Puraye (पुर्ये) in Sangameshwar Taluka and settled down at that place. Puraye was a *watan* given to the Purohit family who supported Bhikajipant and his family. They lived in a small thatched hut. Here he worked on a small agricultural plot. Sale of government stamp paper supplemented his income which was just enough to make both ends meet. The family lived a satisfied life. Bhikajipant's wife, Sagunabai was a soft-spoken lady, efficient in household management, religious in nature and affable. She used to help needy people in the neighbourhood. Because of the helpful nature of the couple they commanded respect from the people in the place.

Bhikajipant had three sons, Mahadeo, Keshav and Ganesh and three daughters, Dhondi, Krishni and Sai. Keshav, the second son, whose name adorns the publishing house, was born on 5 July 1882.

Konkan at that time did not have educational facilities. They were available only in district towns and a few taluka headquarters. Those who were keen to send their children for education to these places had to find some relatives to take care of the young students. Even if some schools were at a reasonable distance, it was not easy to travel this distance. Thus children got the benefit of school education only if such facility was available within a travelable distance. The eldest amongst this family passed his sixth standard and soon got a job as a teacher. His two younger brothers, Keshav and Ganpat were educated up to the third standard.

Keshav Bhikaji spent nearly 16 years at Puraye and helped his father on the farm. He could attend to any hard work due to his robust physique. Totally devoted to his parents and non-complaining in nature, he was satisfied with whatever was available. He never hankered after a luxurious life. Addiction to vices and bad habits was out of question.

Keshav Bhikaji came to Bombay at the request of his elder brother, Mahadeo in 1898. Mahadeo used to run tuition classes. These classes fetched them an adequate income which enabled them to take care of their day-today needs and also contribute to repay debts earlier incurred by Bhikajipant. An interesting episode narrated by Keshav is worth noting. The person who had given a loan to Bhikajipant used to periodically remind him for the repayment of the loan but the other borrowers were not pestered. When the children repaid the entire loan with interest they asked the moneylender about his soft attitude. His reply was typical of a shrewd businessman : "I was sure that you will honour your commitment and will not fail to keep your word once you had given your promise."

Appendix III

Some Noteworthy Specimens in Karnatak Saga

19th century

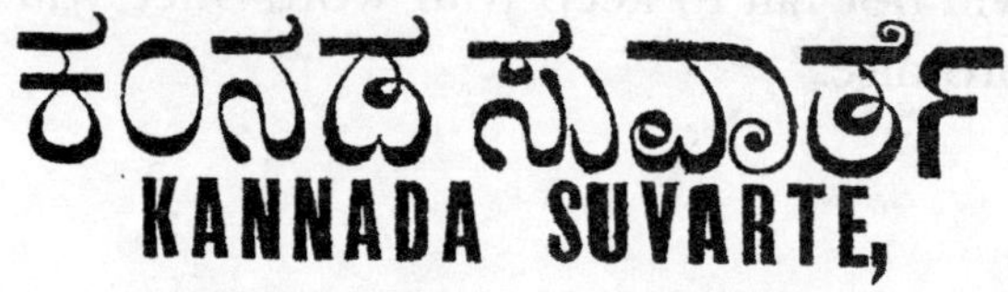

20th century

21st century

Appendix IV

Bibliography

English :

A Caste in a Changing World : The Chitrapur Saraswat Brahmans 1700-1935, Frank E. Conlon, Thomson Press (India) Ltd., New Delhi, 1977

Annual Report on Native Periodicals 1882-1895

Chitrapur Saraswat Directory, H. Shanker Rao (Editor), Kanara Saraswat Association, Mumbai 400007, 1933

Chitrapur Saraswat Miscellanry, H. Shanker Rao (Editor), Kanara Saraswat Association, Mumbai 400007, 1938

Co-operation in India and Abroad : Saraswat Families Part I, Part II, Part III, Rao Bahadur S.S. Talmaki, 1950

Marathi :

त्र्यंबक शंकर शेजवलकर–व्यक्तिमत्त्व आणि कर्तृत्व १८९५-१९६३, सरोजिनी वैद्य (संपादक), कालनिर्णय सांस्कृतिक प्रकाशन, मुंबई, १९९५

कऱ्हेचे पाणी खंड २, १९६४ प्रल्हाद केशव अत्रे, परचुरे प्रकाशन, मुंबई

केशव भिकाजी ढवळे गं. दे. खानोलकर, वा. रा. ढवळे, के. भि. ढवळे, मुंबई

केशव भिकाजी ढवळे-जनशताब्दी स्मरणिका के. भि. ढवळे, मुंबई

एका वाङ्मय सेवकाची शोधयात्रा उषा टाकळकर, गं. दे. खानोलकर स्मृती समिती, मुंबई, २००३

निर्णयसागरची अक्षर साधना पु. ब. कुळकर्णी, निर्णयसागर प्रेस, मुंबई

भारतीय ग्रंथ मुद्रण बापूराव नाईक, कॅ. गो. गं. लिमये ट्रस्ट, पुणे, १९८०

निर्णयसागरची अक्षर साधना : शेट जावजी दादाजी यांचे चरित्र पु. बा. कुळकर्णी निर्णयसागर प्रकाशन, मुंबई, १९६७

सोन्याचे दिवस गं. दे. खानोलकर (संचालक), केशव भिकाजी ढवळे, मुंबई, १९६२

मराठी प्रकाशनाचे स्वरूप, प्रेरणा व परंपरा : पहिले शतक, प्र. द. लिमये, व्हीनस प्रकाशन, पुणे, १९६३

मराठी ग्रंथ सूची खंड १, १९४४, खंड २, १९६१ शंकर गणेश दाते (संपादक), नवीन आवृत्ती प्रकाशक : राज्य मराठी विकास संस्था

मराठी ग्रंथ प्रकाशनाची २०० वर्षे, शरद गोगटे, राजहंस प्रकाशन, पुणे २००८

A Complete Boo

Editorial Department

Art Department

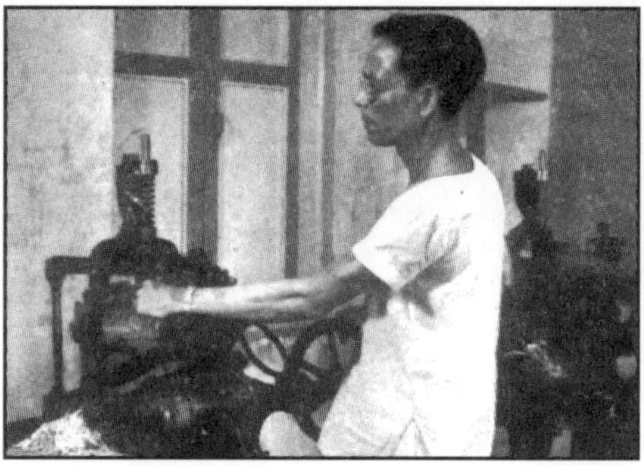

Type Foundry

Composing

Hand-setting

Intertype